To those whose insistent inquiries
and exciting discoveries
have helped elicit and shape
these efforts at affirmation

EVEN SO...
believe

CHESTER A. PENNINGTON

EVEN SO...
believe

ABINGDON PRESS • NASHVILLE • NEW YORK

EVEN SO... BELIEVE

Copyright © 1966 by Abingdon Press

Library of Congress Catalog Card Number: 66-10850

The quotation from *J. B.*, by Archibald MacLeish
(pp. 101-2), is used by permission of Houghton
Mifflin Company

Scripture quotations unless otherwise noted are from the
Revised Standard Version of the Bible, copyrighted 1946
and 1952 by the Division of Christian Education, Na-
tional Council of Churches, and are used by permission.

SET UP, PRINTED, AND BOUND BY THE
PARTHENON PRESS, AT NASHVILLE,
TENNESSEE, UNITED STATES OF AMERICA

foreword

Ours is a time in which, for many persons, faith is difficult. To be sure, there are those for whom faith comes easily. But they are probably the exceptions, even in our churches. For most of us faith comes hard.

A respected, earnest businessman says to me, "I'm just not getting the 'lift' out of my religion that I should be getting."

A thoughtful college student asks, "How can I believe what you teach and still be intellectually honest?"

A troubled young woman cries, "I just can't believe that God loves me. Nobody ever has. If he loves, why is there so little love in my life?"

In the shock of indescribable tragedy, strong men and women groan, "Why?"

The hindrances are there, all right. How will we handle them?

There are difficulties of another sort which frequently limit us to a half-faith.

So a man of great culture and sturdy integrity says to me, "Why don't you get off this theology business? Give us simple religion that will help us in our everyday life. You know that Christianity means following the Golden Rule, living by the Sermon on the Mount." (Incidentally, this is exactly what I don't know!)

This is probably the most widespread and persistent misunderstanding of Christianity in our time. Why shouldn't it be? It is perpetrated by most of the churches. But it is a half-faith, a faith full of neglected hindrances, a faith rendered impotent by its inadequacies. It really can't do much for us. Religious life of this sort has little zip or sparkle. It is a pretty commonplace persistence in moral duty—admirable enough in itself, but hardly what Christianity has claimed to be. And I suspect the reason why we are satisfied to live on such a low level of religious experience is that we hesitate to get involved with difficulties that seem to be beyond our immediate competence.

Personally, I believe the way to an exciting and life-directing faith is not around but straight through such hindrances. And these chapters are attempts to find a way through the hindrances to the helps that are available. This means looking hard at what the hindrances are, resolving those that can be resolved, and learning how to handle those that are unyielding. Such honest dealing with hindrances will yield heartening discovery of helps.

CHESTER A. PENNINGTON

contents

1

THE CLAIM OF REASON /
THE COURAGE TO BELIEVE

"Come now, and let us reason together."

Perhaps the most immediate and obvious hindrance to faith in our particular period of history is the claim of reason—of scientific, analytic reasoning—to be the key to all knowledge. The claim may be easily stated.

This is a pretty amazing universe in which we live. The more we learn about it, the more impressive it appears. Indeed, our capacity to learn seems unlimited. Surely, if our existence has any meaning, we shall be able to discover this by the wise use of our intellectual powers. Whatever truth religion may embody must certainly be discernible to our reason.

We are learning more about human behavior. The science of psychology is disclosing wider and deeper truths about ourselves and furnishing means for the increasing management of ourselves. The social sciences are subjecting interpersonal relations and group activities to similar investigation. We are learning how we act in relation to one another, and perhaps even why. What do we need religion for? The behavioral sciences will tell us all we need to know about ourselves.

And how shall we measure the boundless possibilities of technological knowledge? All the basic necessities of life can now be provided for all men—literally for all men. And not just the necessities either, but a good many niceties as well. Our ability to provide a comfortable life for everyone is unquestioned—if only everyone will accept the rule of reason. Religion, on the other hand, has never distinguished itself at this point. In fact, it has frequently belittled the present life in favor of "pie in the sky." Who needs it? We can have pie and all the trimmings here and now.

So run the arguments. And they are impressive. How shall we affirm the courage to believe?

REASON AND EMOTION

First let us recognize that there really is no sharp separation of the claim of reason from its entanglements in the whole range of our emotions. What we like to think of as the proper insistence of reason may actually be a subtle expression of pride or a stubborn assertion of self-will. We can take apart these elements for the purpose of analysis. But they are all tangled up with each other inside ourselves where we really live. We can think about reason and emotion in separation from each other; but we live them together.

I remember a college professor of psychology under whom I studied. He was one of my ablest and most exciting teachers. He was a staunch champion of behaviorism. He insisted that his position was a strictly reasonable one. But he defended it with such fervor, and his whole demeanor was so charged with emotion, that it was obvious that there was a good deal more than simple intellect involved.

In the course of my association with him, I learned that he had previously been a Baptist preacher. He had carried over into his behavioristic persuasion all the evangelistic fervor of his earlier Baptist belief. I do not question the validity of this. It gave sparkle and vigor to his knowledge. What I do question is his inability to admit that he was emotionally involved in his present position just as much as he had been in his previous persuasion.

He used to say to us students who stubbornly clung to our faith, "I wish I knew what influences you are allowing to persuade you." At the time I had neither the wit nor the wisdom—nor the courage—to reply, "I wish I knew what is influencing you. After all, you are the behaviorist. You are the one who insists that everything we believe and do is strictly determined. What strong influences are persuading you?"

The point is not to criticize the man for being excited about what he believed to be truth. One can admire this. The point is to suggest that our beliefs are not simply rational, that the claims of reason cannot be strictly separated from emotional involvements.

This interrelation is expressed in the verse which forms a biblical statement of the theme of this chapter. The familiar invitation of the prophet is, "Come now, and let us reason together, says the Lord." This sounds fine. But he goes right on to say, "Though your sins are like scarlet, they shall be as white as snow; though they are red like crimson, they shall become like wool" (Isa. 1:18). The invitation to reason becomes a call to repentance!

This is just like the Bible—and may be one reason why many of us avoid it. It slips from reason to repentance. It insists that the beginning of wisdom is the fear of the Lord. It suggests that straight thinking involves considering our relation to God, sensing our moral uncertainty.

Such an approach becomes a hindrance to the person who prides himself on his rationality. The typical modern man does not approach questions of truth in this way. He is likely to say, Let's not get reasoning and repenting mixed up. Modern man likes to suppose that we can think straight even if we are living crooked. Maybe we can—but maybe we can't. At least, we must keep in the back of our minds the possibility that, in order to understand the claim of reason, we may have to do more than just think clearly; we may have to take the risk of faith.

(Somewhere along here a thoughtful reader is going to exclaim, "I wish this fellow would define his terms." Let me reply that there are several meanings to the words "faith" and "reason." What I should like to do is to carry on a conversation with the man of reason, defining terms as we go along, to whatever extent clarity requires, and trying not to get too impassioned about the subject of reason!)

REASON AND FAITH

The claim of reason is frequently reflected in the apparent conflict between science and religion. This is a perennial issue in modern religious thought. It has been a troublemaker for a couple of centuries. It recurs every generation, and never more dramatically than in our own. We all are aware of the fabulous range of scientific knowledge. There appears to be no limit to the potential of scientific discovery. What does this do to the claims of religion?

Does the increase of knowledge reduce and perhaps eliminate the need for religious belief? My reply is that, if the religious claim is properly understood, it remains valid not just in spite of but precisely in relation to the increase of knowledge.

It is commonly supposed that we need belief in God in order to explain what we cannot otherwise understand. That is, if we can explain an event or process scientifically, we no longer need appeal to God in that specific regard.

For instance, in other centuries men have believed that lightning was the expression of the wrath of an annoyed deity. We know today that it is due to certain kinds of electrical charges, acting under certain atmospheric conditions. We do not blame lightning on an angry God. Nor do we, as a friend puts it, blame the frost that kills our cabbage on an angry God. So with other natural phenomena. As we explain them scientifically, we no longer need to explain them with reference to God.

There is no apparent end to what we can discover and understand scientifically. Therefore, the argument goes, we really don't need belief in God.

This point of view rests on a false understanding of the religious claim. We do not believe in God simply as a hypothesis to explain what we do not know or what we cannot discover. We believe in God as the Origin and Sustainer of all that we know, as well as what we do not know. God does not live in the diminishing gaps of our knowledge. If God is, he exists as the Ground of our whole existence. Indeed, the very process of learning is itself an expression of his purpose. The increase of our knowledge is the exercise of his gift of reason. As thoughtful men of an earlier generation used to say, "The reason of man is the candle of the Lord." What we discover, by the use of his gift, are his manifold ways of sustaining life in our world. And as we discover these, we are able to use them for the further increase of knowledge and the enrichment of life.

For instance, we are assured that researchers are right on the verge of "creating" life in a test tube. This will certainly be a most impressive achievement. Some people are worried about the religious implications of this. They reason that if man can create life, why do we need to believe in God any more? We have imagined that the act of creation is a divine prerogative. If man succeeds in bringing about the conditions which make life possible in a test tube, they suppose, faith in God is seriously threatened.

I quite fail to see any real threat in such a challenge —and for two reasons. In the first place, in discovering how life originates, we are simply uncovering a process which has been going on for countless ages. In fact, I am not sure we are really "creating" anything. What we are doing is putting together elements which are already at hand. We are taking apart—and then putting together again—the process by which life has been brought about and sustained from the beginning of time. There is a very real sense in which what we are doing is what God has been doing endlessly. And I see in this no threat to faith in God. It would be sheer presumption to imagine that what we may do for a moment in a tiny tube is sufficient to "explain" the entire cosmic process upon which we are utterly dependent.

Second, the most remarkable aspect of this whole discovery is not what happens in the test tube. It is the purposive and creative mind that has made possible the achievement. This is one of the things that disturbs me about much so-called philosophy of science. We become so intent upon the scientific processes themselves that we overlook the creative and imaginative mind that is investigating and sometimes originating these processes. The origin of life in a test tube would be utterly impossible without the long, patient, creative work of the minds of the men who are carrying forward this project. What is most remarkable, therefore, is not what happens in the test tube, but the creative process that starts in the mind of man and makes the physical process possible.

Some of us believe that this is an impressive analogy to what must be true in the universe itself. In the universe there appears not only life, but self-conscious life, creatures who know themselves to exist. More remarkable than that, these creatures look at and investigate the very process that has produced them. For some of us the presence of this kind of being in the universe implies the presence of cosmic purpose, of creative intent, in the very nature of things.

Be that as it may, the point I want to make is that the claim of religious faith is not threatened by increasing knowledge. If God is, he exists as the Ground, the Origin, the Sustainer of the whole process of existence. A direct way of saying it would be this. Rub out the world, and God still is. Rub out God, and there is nothing.

Reason will continue to press its claim: But can you prove the existence of God? No matter how learnedly some philosophers and theologians may argue that the question has no meaning in this form, this is the way most people ask it.

The strange fact is that usually the challenger will not accept the sort of evidence which the believer offers. There is always an alternative to every reason given for the existence of God. There are some perfectly good arguments for the reality of God. They may be quite impressive to the believer. But the skeptic will not accept a single one. The unbeliever—or rather, the believer in no-God—is quite unimpressed by any argument put forward by the believer in God.

We simply have to say that there is no strictly scientific proof, no evidence acceptable to the analytic mind, where religious truths are at stake. We can't pin God down and examine him, like a frog sprawled on a lab table. We can't measure deity on a psychograph, or make a smear for study under a microscope. Whatever we get by these means, it certainly is not deity. The evidence for religious truths is of another kind.

We all remember, some time ago, when the Russian cosmonaut went spinning around the world for several days. On coming down to earth, he reported that he had seen no signs of God out there. This may seem impudent and naive. But it is only a rather obvious form of the argument frequently used by many skeptics: We don't see any evidence for your beliefs.

To this we simply have to reply that the assurance of faith is not scientific proof. Indeed, we would say that religious assurance is deeper than rational certainty. It is a knowledge given to the whole person, not simply to the intellect. A knowledge that becomes deeper the more we live it.

Actually, most of the affirmations of Christian faith have nothing to do with scientific reasoning—and vice versa. Whether Jesus was the Son of God is not a scientific question. Whether Jesus was born of a virgin cannot be argued on biological grounds alone. Just how Jesus was raised from the dead is not a problem for the historians. These are affirmations of faith—and their proper science is theology.

What historical knowledge can verify is that faith in Jesus as the Christ is clearly the faith of the New Testament. Research can help us discover some of the events and processes by which that faith developed, and what consequences it had in history. But whether this affirmation is true cannot be touched by history or by any other science. It is truth of another kind.

REASON AND ITS LIMITS

The challenge of reason is usually based on a more fundamental claim: that technical reason is the final judge of what is true and false, real and illusory. This assertion may take several forms. Some men will appeal to scientific method as the only way to discover truth.

Others will use the psychological argument that religious belief is "projection" or "wish-fulfillment." Others will prearrange their standards of what is philosophically admissible—and lo, the theistic arguments do not fit. What it all comes to is the basic assumption that analytic and technical reason is the only arbiter of truth.

The Christian faith flatly states that this claim is presumptuous. To say that the human reason, unaided, is the sole and final judge of all truth is an act of faith that goes beyond any rightful claim. As a matter of fact, we would say, there are human experiences quite beyond the grasp of scientific reason—experiences of emotion, insight, wonder—that reason itself must take into account as evidences of truth.

Every serious Christian thinker I know anything about has insisted that our reason is limited. And it may be that there is no way to be a Christian without acknowledging such limitations.

There are several ways of saying this. Let me start with the least attractive, most irritating way.

Christian thinkers have historically said that reason is corrupted by sin, just as all our powers are. If we are sinners—and the Christian faith has never doubted this—then every aspect of our life shares this dislocation, including our ability to think. Therefore, it stands to reason that we can expect our minds to be incapable of penetrating all the secrets of life. Moreover, sensing our limitation, we will quite understandably react by claiming too much for our own powers. We know very well that we do this all the time; it is a perfectly familiar psychological phenomenon known as "compensation" or "defensiveness." It is not at all unreasonable to suggest that we do this with respect to our basic power of reason. Sensing that we really are limited in our capacity to know, we claim that there is no limit to our ability to know. The first demand of honesty may be to admit our limitations.

However, such an admission does not come easily. The very suggestion of it is offensive to us, for reasons we may have to look into more deeply. We do not want to confess that our reason is seriously limited by anything remotely connected with the notion of sin. So it may be helpful to find other ways of saying this which may not raise our defenses quite so quickly.

Certainly the Freudian and post-Freudian insights would suggest that there is a good deal more to our lives than the rational. That there are profound emotional and unconscious components in our lives is now a commonplace. Some schools of thought are willing to reckon seriously with this fact, some are not. But it seems clear that the successful life requires that we bring into good working relation the rational and irrational elements of our being. And is it unreasonable to suggest that these irrational elements may disclose truths about ourselves which the rational must take into account?

Similarly, it seems reasonable to suggest that there

are experiences in life which go beyond the strictly analytic reason. The miracle of love is more than a biological reaction. The experience of beauty is more than an intellectual exercise and so is the still more mysterious creation of beauty. The apprehension of meaning is probably larger than bare thinking. And the religious man would say that the intuitions of religion are also more than simply rational.

We must either define reason to include these aspects of our experience, or admit that analytic reason in itself is limited and needs help from these other experiences.

Among our contemporaries, Paul Tillich probably addresses himself most eloquently to this issue. He speaks, first of all, of the finitude of reason. After all, we are finite creatures. And if there is an infinite, it is clear that we are limited in our capacity to grasp it or him or whatever we should call the infinite. But Tillich goes on to speak further of our estrangement, both from the universe which is our home and from our own true nature. Therefore, if we are to learn the truth about ourselves and our world, we must be open to disclosures which may come to us. We must be teachable, willing to accept truths or insights which we do not discover but which disclose themselves to us. Christianity calls this process "revelation."

Now there need not be—and here it is the writer, not Tillich, speaking—anything "miraculous" about this. These revelations may come through our relations with other persons, or through everyday experiences which we do not necessarily think of as "religious." But to men of faith, this is revelation. In and through these revelatory experiences we may believe that God is disclosing the truth about himself, the world, ourselves.

In whatever ways we may say it, we must recognize the limitation of reason as such. There are some truths in life which we cannot discover by exclusively rational investigation. We must be open to the whole range of experience.

But we must also recognize the proper place of reason. Reason does have a role to play in faith. And a genuine faith will be glad to make the best use of reason.

If reason is limited, so also is faith. If reason is corrupted, so also is our capacity for believing. Faith may become arrogant and go far beyond its proper domain. The person who defiantly believes what he has been taught in church, regardless of scientific evidence, is not necessarily a man of faith.

In fact, the New Testament meaning of the word "faith" is not the acceptance of propositions, or the knowledge of facts. Faith means our encounter with God. Faith means our confidence that God comes to meet us in Jesus Christ. Faith means that I rush to meet him who comes to meet me. Faith means the commitment of myself to the One who gives himself for me. Incidentally, in the New Testament the opposite of faith is not doubt but sin. So that faith does not mean making all kinds of assertions about the world as scientifically understood, or insisting upon certain supposed facts. Faith means standing in the proper relation to God.

If we are to think of faith as knowledge, it is more like knowledge of ourselves and of other persons, rather than the knowledge of facts. We know God not as we know algebra or geography or electronics but as we know one another.

So there are some of us who believe that faith is not the enemy of reason, nor need reason be the antagonist of faith. Reason does have an important part to play in the development of a mature faith. An intelligent faith will make the best possible use of reason. Reason is fulfilled in faith; and faith needs reason for its self-understanding.

A REASONABLE FAITH

What are some of the things we dare reasonably to believe?

Always and everywhere, God has been seeking to reveal himself. It is of his very nature to give himself; so that always and everywhere he has been striving to make himself known to men. But we humans suffer from various kinds of limitations. God cannot always get through. The varieties of religions are expressive of our incapacity to receive or accept, and God's incapacity to break through our resistance.

But at one point, God was able to break through with a clarity and definitiveness which he achieved nowhere else. He, Infinite Person, was able to reveal himself in a person whom we know as Jesus the Christ. It is in Jesus Christ that we see most clearly revealed the character and purpose of God.

If we will open ourselves to this act of God in Christ, we will be seized by the truth which he reveals. We will be empowered with the grace which he gives. And we will be drawn into ever deeper understanding of ourselves and of God and of our world. We will grow into increasing maturity and fulfillment.

This is our faith. We believe this with all of our life. And reason gives assent. Indeed, in this faith reason and all the powers of our being find fulfillment.

2

THE RELUCTANCE OF PRIDE /
THE ADMISSION OF NEED

"All have sinned and fall short."

One of Abraham Lincoln's favorite quotations was a verse beginning, "Oh, why should the spirit of mortal be proud?" The poem is a meditation on our mortality: life is short; generations come and go in quick sucession; so why should we be proud? But man *is* proud—proud at least of being human—and not without reason.

The creative and inventive achievements of man are considerable. Man possesses magnificent powers and gifts. So there is a long and respected tradition of humanism which celebrates the uniqueness of man. This is well summarized in the words of Shakespeare:

> What a piece of work is a man! how noble in reason! how infinite in faculty! in form and moving how express and admirable! in acting how like an angel! in apprehension how like a god! the beauty of the world! the paragon of animals! (Hamlet, Act II, scene ii)

Such recognition of the distinctiveness of man can also be expressed within a religious context. So the psalmist, praising God, celebrates man.

> When I look at thy heavens, the
>   work of thy fingers,
>   the moon and the stars which
>   thou hast established;
> what is man that thou art mindful
>   of him,
>   and the son of man that thou
>   dost care for him?
> Yet thou has made him little less
>   than God,
>   and dost crown him with glory
>   and honor.
> Thou has given him dominion over
>   the works of thy hands;
>   thou hast put all things under his
>   feet (Ps. 8:3-6).

"The paragon of animals!",

"Little less than God!"

We may say both.

What then is the danger of pride? The Greeks knew, and they had a word for it. Pride becomes dangerous, they said—even fatal—when a man lifts himself up against the gods, defies their will, and challenges his own fate. This was the error of the heroes of Greek tragedy. They proudly defied fate, but were crushed by it.

In biblical language, pride becomes destructive when

28

man forgets that his capacities are the gift of God and that he is dependent upon God for the exercise of whatever powers he is granted. So the very psalm which salutes man concludes, "O Lord, our Lord, how majestic is thy name in all the earth!" A British poet of the nineteenth century put it quite differently: "Glory to man in the highest; for man is the master of things!" The conclusion of faith is, "Glory to God, who has so graciously made us to have dominion over his creation."

I occasionally think of these contrasts when reading of our exploits in space. Here is an extraordinary expression of the almost incredible powers of man. There are doubtless limits to what we can do, but we are pushing them back all the time. And what we *can* do is impressive enough. Yet I sometimes wonder if this may be a final, unwitting assertion of human pride. Occasionally our attitude seems to be, "See how great we are! If we apply ourselves to it, we can conquer anything!" And I think I hear a taunting reply, "Anything? What about yourself, man?"

However this may be, there is reason to suspect that one of the primary hindrances to faith is just this kind of pride. The Greek hero did not know that he suffered from a tragic flaw. He could not see his own weakness. And his blindness was due to his defiant pride. Modern man is not inclined to admit his inability to solve his own problems. But Christian faith demands just such an admission. Faith is impossible without a recognition of need. But we are reluctant to make such a confession.

We continue to insist that we can solve our own problems. And the attitude underlying our insistence is not a coolly reasoned certainty. It is an implicit pride.

PARADOXES OF PRIDE

For the past four hundred years or so, ever since Copernicus, we have known that the earth is not the center of the universe. More recently we have learned just how vast the universe really is. Correspondingly, we have become impressed with the insignificance of man. It has become commonplace in our time to recognize that man is an infinitesimally tiny figure, struggling to maintain his existence on the thin crust of an insignificant little ball in a tiny galaxy in an enormous universe.

Now the ironic fact is that, with a great show of wisdom, we are willing to admit the insignificance of man in the face of a vast universe. But for some strange reason we are reluctant to admit that we are insignificant before almighty God. Now why is this? Why are we so willing, almost eager, to affirm that in the universe we amount to practically nothing? But we are utterly unwilling to say that before God, if we amount to anything, it is his grace that makes it so.

I think the reason is not an intellectual one. It is sheer pride. We would rather admit that we are un-important in a vast, impersonal cosmos, which we can defy, though not ultimately. But we cannot bring our-selves to confess that there is an Infinite Person before whom we are as nothing, except as he makes us something.

There is an inconsistency even in the admission we do make. Not long ago I read an article in which the author confidently affirmed, "Man can no longer think of himself as central to the purpose of the universe." This sounds learned, and is clearly aimed at the religious view of man. But the writer goes on to say that the most important question in the universe right now is precisely what man will do with his new knowledge. So the author has succeeded in affirming what he has just denied. The human creature may no longer be central, but he possesses an extraordinary power by which he can render life—at least in this corner of the universe—impossible. The religious man would assert that this power gives the human creature a strange centrality in cosmic purposes, and that this is rooted in his relation to the creator of the universe himself.

The paradox remains. Why are we so willing to say, "Before the universe, we are as nothing," and on the other hand so unwilling to say, "Before God, we are as nothing"? The only answer which carries any conviction to me is our pride.

Another illustration can be found in the insights of contemporary psychology, which has uncovered all sorts of dark and ugly facts about us humans. Ask any psychoanalyst to describe what he finds lurking in our subconscious minds. And if you don't like psychoanalysis, ask almost any school of psychology to describe human motivation and behavior. They will tell you a story of devious and destructive ways. The recital of our capacity for deception, hate, lust for power is a lengthy one. We will resort to all kinds of learned vocabulary to describe these aspects of our human experience. But when the Christian faith suggests that they may be expressions of what has been known as sin, we reject the notion as hopelessly outmoded. Why? We will confess to all sorts of unconscious compulsions, confused emotions, social errors. But we are reluctant to confess that we are sinners before God. Why? We are just too proud.

Another expression of such pride is to be found in the foreword to Arthur Miller's play *After the Fall*. Incidentally, we should pay attention to the title. It is very significant. Such titles do not happen by accident; they are deliberately chosen. And Arthur Miller is saying that our human condition can be described as the sequel to some mythic fall. The protagonist of the play has failed to be a real person. He has spoiled his own life and the lives of those who are involved with him. He is "weighed down with a sense of his own pointlessness and the world's." He is a "fallen man." And we are asked to see our own condition in his plight.

Yet we must inquire more closely into this notion of the fall. We know its mythic origins. It happens to be found in the Bible. But as Miller uses it, what does it mean? Fall from what? Fall before whom? And here the playwright has done a remarkable thing. He has eliminated any cosmic dimension (God, in Genesis) from the myth. The "Listener" in the play is the protagonist himself. The action takes place within his own mind. So there is no one over against the Man, Quentin, or Adam, or ourselves. He has fallen in front of himself!

This can be nothing other than the author's deliberate interpretation of the original story of Adam, which gives the play its title. He has cut out the crucial dimension of the fall. The Genesis account indicates with unmistakable clarity that the fall occurs before the Creator, that man falls away from a divine intention, and that this is the root of the human tragedy. To eliminate this cannot be accidental. Miller knows what he is doing, and he means something by it.

Martin Luther somewhere describes our human condition in an interesting phrase: "The heart turned in upon itself." This is a perfect description of the leading character in Miller's play. He is shut up to discuss his interior problems with no one but himself. But for Luther, as for all Christian thinkers, this condition is a consequence of our fall away from God.

One is forced to ask why Miller and so many other sensitive artists in our time reject the clear meaning of the ancient myth. We recognize the intellectual difficulties which stand in the way of faith. We appreciate the fact that these artists are sensitive to these hindrances. But I cannot help thinking there is a further dimension in their reluctance to admit this meaning. They see so clearly the ambiguities and anxieties of our condition. Yet they are reluctant to confess that we are sprawled in a grotesque posture before the One to whom we owe our very being. And I believe that one word for this reluctance is pride.

Interestingly enough, some of the most sensitive interpreters of the Christian faith in our time insist that exactly this kind of pride is the basic sin of man. Sin is not some naughty act, such as sneaky sex. Sin is precisely this proud lifting up of ourselves over against God. It is our will to seize responsibility for our condition, with our unwillingness to confess that this is a responsibility exercised before God. Driven out of Eden, we need no swords in the hands of angels to keep us out. All we need is our stubborn pride, which prevents our returning to the intention for which we were made. It is this pride which is our original sin.

With uncomfortable honesty, the Christian faith presses the claim that we can never really know ourselves until we recognize ourselves as sinners before God, erring rebels, lost and trying to find our own way. We shall never know the creative and renewing power of God until we admit our desperate need of him. So the Christian faith insists that pride be surrendered, that we confess our need, and yield ourselves to the loving purpose of God.

PARABLES OF OUR PREDICAMENT

Such statements as those just made are apt to be received skeptically, or perhaps rejected outright. "They don't communicate," we say, implying that the terms themselves no longer carry meaning to our generation. So we must try other ways of portraying our predicament. It may be that these other pictures will not communicate either. We may remain unconvinced.

Is it fair to raise the possibility that some of our difficulty with "communication" in this area is our reluctance to hear what is being said? May it be that we just do not want to admit such things about ourselves? We may try every means of communication open to us. But we must remember that this is a two-way process. We must be willing to get the message.

Any description of our human condition today must resort to such terms as anxiety, guilt, fear, loneliness, estrangement. The deepest insights of psychology say to all of us that we are threatened by these profound emotions. They have become everyday words in the lexicon of self-understanding. Let us consider only the first of these.

Most serious students of man are convinced that one of the deepest marks of our existence is that we are threatened by anxiety. Not only do the technical scholars and therapists tell us this, but also the dramatists and novelists—and with great eloquence.

Many of you will simply shrug and say, "Who, me?

35

I'm not aware of any particular anxiety." To which they will reply, "Of course, you are not aware of it. That's just the point. Are you willing to let down your guard long enough to sense the impact of this? Will you look behind the front which you put up for others—and which sometimes fools you too?"

Most of us have learned to cope with these feelings in one way or other. So perhaps the claim should be stated a little differently. Unless you have been fortunate enough to find in your life an honest, freely given, healing love, you are likely to be driven by a deep anxiety you do not even know you have. Unless you have faced this and learned to handle it, you are likely to be profoundly uneasy about life, without knowing why.

What are some of the factors which tend to make us anxious? First we could mention the basic insecurity of life, whether in terms of economics or mortality. We put in a good bit of time and effort trying to reduce economic insecurity. This has become a great political as well as fiscal concern. But there is one insecurity which we can never eliminate, and that is the certainty of death. We are working in a determined way to reduce or eliminate many serious diseases. But no matter how successful we may be, there will always be one that will get us in the end. There simply is no way of eliminating this basic insecurity.

Another cause of anxiety may be our difficulties in getting along with others. There are always some people we do not like or cannot get along with. And for many people there are secret, seldom admitted tensions and maladjustments in family life.

Then there are those deeply hidden, unadmitted personal inadequacies, which no one else knows but ourselves. We carry this secret knowledge within us, and it makes us uneasy.

The most frequent reaction to these insecurities is to try to hide them under a flurry of activities. Some people work very hard and seldom let up. They just won't take time to sit and think. Other people specialize in letting up. Most entertainment is either a distraction or an anesthetic. We have to do something to keep our mind off our uneasiness, or at least dull its discomfort.

Is there anything here you recognize? In yourself, that is. Most of us manage to keep a pretty tight grip upon ourselves and will not allow these feelings to be deeply sensed. But is there anyone who has not occasionally felt the ground shake beneath his feet? Is there anyone who has not sometimes felt as if he were standing on the edge of an abyss and not quite sure whether he could keep his balance? The Christian faith has something to say about this sense of balance, which depends primarily on what—or who—is at the center of your life.

The biblical understanding of our insecure posture is stated directly in the unpleasantly familiar words of Paul: "All have sinned and fall short of the glory of God" (Rom. 3:23). Fall short of what? Of God's creative intention for us. He made us to be one thing. We have turned out to be something else. But you will say that is only human. Of course it is. That is exactly the problem. For in saying this, we do not offer an excuse; we only provide a description. To be human is to fall short of the divine intention.

In other words, the Christian faith asserts that the anxiety which lies near the core of our being is really an expression of a still deeper condition—our uneasiness before God.

It is not easy for us to accept such a judgment. We are respectable members of the church and community. Our personal lives are decent and well adjusted, at least as far as public knowledge is concerned. Only we ourselves know the private exceptions to our public reputations. Still we are reluctant to accept the notion that we are sinners before God.

Part of the difficulty may lie in the old-fashioned word "sin." This term is usually understood to mean certain kinds of undesirable behavior. For instance, we think a murderer or an adulterer is obviously a sinner. But we are neither of these, and we do not want to be classified with them.

The Bible, however, is much more careful in its use of the word "sin." Sin is not simply some wrong deed that we do; it is what is wrong with us that makes us do it. We are not sinners because we sin; we sin because we are sinners. We do wrong because there is something wrong with us. And what is wrong is our strained relation with God.

We are neither willing nor able to keep God really and exclusively first in our lives. In the course of our development as persons, we become self-centered. In our pride, we presume to live our lives in our own way, for our own purposes. We may ask God to bless us in our self-directed decisions. But he certainly cannot enter into this kind of arrangement. So the relation between us is strained.

We may go on as if everything were fine. We prefer to think it is. After all, we are not doing anything terribly bad. Life is pretty good to us. God can't expect too much; we are only human. We even go through the approved exercises of religion, being assured that this will smooth over anything that may have gone wrong.

But the Christian faith is disturbingly clear. Our relations with God do not grow out of or depend upon our respectability or any of the characteristics which society values. Every last one of us has disarranged his relation with God. And unless we have let him set it to rights, we are sinners before him.

We are strangely mixed creatures: made "a little lower than God," we are capable of incredible depravity; made to be the children of God, we are torn by the powers shared with our fellow animals; haunted by the memory of our origins in the creative will of God, we are tragically hurt by our fall from this high purpose.

PROMISE OF PARDON

The true measure of the greatness of man is the admission of our need for divine restoration. The promise of the gospel is that, if we will accept the forgiveness which God freely offers, he will restore us to our proper status ("glory").

The most serious consequence of pride is that it blocks us from accepting the pardon and renewal which God offers. In our anxious reluctance to admit our need, even our religion becomes an exercise in self-deception. The anxiety and guilt which we do not recognize tend to do one or both of two things to our understanding of God.

On the one hand, because of our deeply felt but unrecognized guilt, we may find it impossible to believe that God really forgives us. We think that he requires a certain moral excellence (and we can never be too sure whether we qualify), plus religious practices (which we follow with interruptions). So we can never be really sure we are forgiven. How can we know? We don't feel any different.

On the other hand, in our anxiety we may do exactly the opposite. We may sentimentalize God and reduce the apparent need for forgiveness. First of all, we discard the notion of eternal punishment. If God is love, we say, he does not want anyone to get hurt. He will see that everything turns out all right. But this is phony, and we know it. We can have no genuine respect for a deity who will let us get away with anything. So this sort of sentimentality does not really ease our anxieties. We go on coddling our guilt, and are uneasy about it. And we fail to understand why.

The true promise of the gospel reaches much deeper than these efforts at self-justification. Paul states it in a classic affirmation: "God was in Christ reconciling the world to himself" (II Cor. 5:19). That is, God comes to us in Christ, precisely to disarm our pride, to break down the barrier we have built up against him, to get through the front we have put up around ourselves. God does not wait for us to make the first move. He takes the initiative in trying to show us the roots of our anxiety, to disclose the defensiveness of our partly sensed guilt. And he keeps the initiative, enacting the true nature of his self-giving love, his unchanging will to pardon our proud withdrawal, to restore our proper posture before him.

We may be released from anxious pride and given the assurance of pardon. This promise is fulfilled as we admit the seriousness of our condition and accept the divine offer of restoration. Jesus indicated this in one of his most famous stories (Luke 18:9ff).

Two men went up to the temple to pray. One was self-assured, confident of his moral character and his religious status. He prayed—quite honestly—"God, I thank thee." He meant this. He had much for which to be thankful, and he knew it.

The other man had no confidence in his own position

41

or achievement. The best prayer he could muster was, "God, be merciful to me, a sinner." But, Jesus said, it was this man who returned to his home forgiven, restored to his proper place as a son of God, confident in his renewed relation to God.

3

THE CHALLENGE OF SELF-WILL /
THE DEMAND FOR OBEDIENCE

"If ye love me, keep my commandments."

Consider the paradox of self-will. You have to have it, in order to become a person; but to become a fulfilled person, you have to get over it. This two-sided truth has many important implications for our faith.

I remember the first time our first child deliberately defied me. I don't remember the occasion, what prompted it, or what happened after it. But I remember the impact this primordial event had on me.

There is every reason to believe that our daughter knew from her earliest days that her parents loved her, that they willed only her good. Yet there came a time when she—tiny creature—looked up at me with eyes which everyone says look strangely like my own, and said flatly, NO.

Suddenly I heard an echo from Eden. This was not one man's child; this was Eve. This was not my daughter and her father; this was myself and God. And I said inwardly, "What your daughter has done to you is just what you have done to God. You know he loves you. You know he wills only your good. Yet you have looked at him with eyes which scripture says look strangely like his own, and you have said, NO."

There is no better illustration of the mixed nature of man than this: self-will is necessary but must also be transcended. In the very process of becoming a person, each one of us must assert himself and his own will to be himself. The person who develops no will of his own, but is at the mercy of other people and outside influences, is not much of a person. But unless this self-will is modified, we become self-centered, which is a particularly miserable kind of immaturity. If we are to become mature persons, experiencing some sense of fulfillment, we must transcend self-centeredness. We must get beyond ourselves. We must find our will caught up in some larger, wider purpose than our own self-interest.

Most of us are willing to accept these propositions. Yet we must also recognize that, once we get a will of our own, we do not easily surrender it. And at this point, the demand of faith runs headlong into our willfulness. Faith demands our willingness to put the will of God above our own will. Faith demands that we surrender our will to God's will. But we resist. This is the ultimate surrender. We do not easily make it. And much that we call disbelief may really be the assertion of self-will.

THE FORMATION OF THE WILL

The way most of us are conventionally reared, it doesn't take us long to get the impression that God is a kind of cosmic law enforcement officer. Whether this understanding is true is, for the moment, beside the point. This is a later and more sophisticated question. The fact seems to be that, as we grow up, we are given to understand that there is a God who sets up the rules of right and wrong, and whose business it is to enforce them. It also happens that we do not always like these rules and do not particularly want to obey them.

The chief representatives of God, of course, are our parents. We early learn—whether justly or not—that it is God who makes up the rule that we should obey our parents. "Honor thy father and thy mother" has the sound of ultimate authority. It never occurs to us, until later, that this command might be a parental invention. No. We learn that the words came down from heaven by way of an awe-inspiring figure with strange tablets of stone under his arm. So there is formed in us the conviction that behind this law and several other annoying restrictions stands God, who is the law-giver and the enforcement officer.

At almost the same time we become aware of a tendency to rebel against, or at least to challenge, authority. What we do not realize is that we are acquiring a will of our own. As we do so, we find ourselves in conflict with the will of our parents. Before we know it, we are testing our will over against theirs. And it is not long before our culture, or maybe something deep within ourselves, is telling us that we are in rebellion against God.

It is important for us to notice that this defiance is not a rational decision to which the child comes by the process of cool deliberation. The child does not sit down and say, "I think I will rebel against my parents. What's a good way to start?" Actually, the child is in rebellion against his parents before he knows it. By the time he becomes aware of himself, he is already setting his will up over against their will. This is what it means to become a person. And the child, without knowing it, is bent on asserting his will to be.

Not long ago, I was talking with some of my parishioners about what is traditionally known as original sin. They considered this—as do many nice people —an unpleasant, distasteful notion. The doctrine may merit both adjectives. But it may also be an accurate description of reality. So I tried to express it in terms of this necessary self-centeredness which is part of our becoming a person, but which is also an aspect of our personality which has to be disciplined and modified. They kept pressing me with two observations. One, it is only human. To which I could only reply, "Of course. To be human is to be a rebel, to be a sinner." But, they continued, when does this begin? And I suggested that by the time a child becomes aware of himself he knows himself to be already in rebellion against God.

Striking confirmation of this is given in Arthur Miller's foreword to *After the Fall*. He interprets the biblical account of man as saying that "the human being becomes 'himself' in the act of becoming aware of his sinfulness. He 'is' what he is ashamed of." The author suggests that we only come to know ourselves "after the fall." And at the conclusion of the play the protagonist accepts the insight that we only come to know one another "after the fall." This is exactly what the Christian faith has always contended.

Our first child's first rebellion seems to be a fitting parable of what I am trying to say. Her act of defiance was both necessary and responsible. Some logically minded person may say that an act cannot be both necessary and responsible. But life declares that this insight is deeper than logic and entirely valid. This universal, primeval deed of my daughter was inevitable. Yet the doer had to be held responsible for what had been done.

The act was necessary in the sense that it was essential to her becoming a person. If she were ever to be a person in her own right, she simply had to come to the place where she asserted herself over against her parents. Indeed, her parents really wanted this to happen. And, thank God, it did.

But now she also had to assume responsibility for the act and its consequences. This defiance, necessary as it was, could not be allowed to go unnoticed, unchallenged, unpunished. This assertion of self-will, and all those which followed, required definition, direction, discipline.

This is the way we become persons—by finding ourselves, by discovering that we have a will of our own, by asserting that will. This is also exactly the way we become sinners. Are the two the same? To become a person is to become a sinner?

THE FRUSTRATION OF THE WILL

We can agree that self-will is important and necessary and good. We must also recognize that our will to be ourselves is easily betrayed in unexpected ways. We are naturally on our guard against domination by the will of someone else. We are not so quick to see that the will to be somebody can be frustrated in two ways that are commonly regarded as socially desirable.

First of all, self-will easily deteriorates into conformity with popularly accepted practices. That is, we grow up in a particular civilization, which values certain goals, gives status to certain ways of behavior. It is easy—it even seems desirable—to go along with what our civilization approves. And if religious teaching presumes to challenge the popular codes, we are inclined to go along with our group. In the name of personal freedom, we stoutly defend our right to be a slave to conformity.

It is rather sad to see the way in which people, in the

name of their independence, will meekly conform to the pressures and demands of their in-group. This is particularly evident if the church challenges these mores. Not that the teachings of the church must always be equated with the will of God. But let's imagine that a person's church is questioning a particular social custom, or number of customs, in the name of a higher allegiance to the will of God. People will often say indignantly, "I'm not going to let the church or the preacher tell me what to do!" And they shouldn't, of course. The sad irony is that they have already let the hucksters and the taste-makers tell them what to do.

What is required is genuine self-determination, that is, the will to stand over against the persuasions of society, the standards of popular culture, and determine for one's self the values and aims to which one will direct his powers. And not quite incidentally, this is the best way to discover what is the will of God.

It must be confessed, somewhat reluctantly, that a certain kind of youthful rebellion turns out to be just such conformity to the requirements of adolescent society. One says this with genuine understanding, but also with the hope that young people might be willing to face up to such a possibility. Are they really rebelling against their parents, their upbringing, or are they simply conforming to the popular pressures of the moment?

The real challenge to youth is the same as that to their elders—to resist the pressures to conform, to take an honest look at the prevailing practices, and then to decide whether one wants to accept these standards or affirm others. This means to evaluate these conventions against which one is expected to rebel, not just to discard them unthinkingly. The latter is mere conformity and not the discovery of the self.

Unwilling to surrender to the will of God, many of us have already surrendered to the will of society. Lacking the courage to respond to the demand of faith, we have yielded to the pressures of our culture. Self-will has become conformity. And there is no fulfillment of the self in this sort of surrender.

The second way in which self-will may be frustrated is to become centered in one's self. Self-will becomes self-centeredness. And this too is frustration.

Jesus said this is his own way: He who tries to hold on to his own life will lose it; but he who is willing to lose his life for the sake of something greater will find himself. If you live only for yourself, you will be stifled by frustration and emptiness. Self-centered goals are not big enough to evoke and satisfy all the powers of the self.

Nor are family-centered goals sufficient. Many men and women are spending themselves for the sake of their children. But this can also be subtly self-centered. In any case, it is not sufficient to yield genuine self-realization. Many persons are frustrated and restless because they are spending themselves frantically for their families. And this can yield no sufficient satisfaction. Self-will must find its fulfillment in being expended for larger goals and purposes than those which center in or circle about the self.

There is considerable evidence that much of the frenzied sex behavior in our time is not simply a breakdown of moral standards, but rather a breaking out of frustrated self-will. People frantically try to find themselves without surrendering themselves. One young man is quoted as saying, "Sex is domination. Love is surrender. Who wants to surrender?" That way lies madness, the breakdown of the self. The will to devour others is itself devoured. (Cf. Gal. 5:15.)

Self-centeredness is loneliness, isolation. We try to break out of this by establishing connections with someone else. We want to do this without really yielding ourselves to anyone. So we resort to the most obvious and exciting connection—sex. And it turns out to be a frighteningly lonely thing.

Tennessee Williams, in *Night of the Iguana,* speaks of our searching for "broken gates between people so that they can reach each other, even if it's for one night only." And, he continues, how often we learn "how lonely the intimate connection can be."

Interestingly enough, this is almost exactly paralleled in a contemporary novel, in which the author comments on certain kinds of frenzied sexual behavior. "The common denominator is loneliness . . . a momentary sharing of sex. And beyond that the infinite separation, the alienation."

The end of self-will, centered upon itself, is frustration.

THE FULFILLMENT OF THE WILL

These considerations lead us to make a strong positive claim. It may be true that there is a sharp collision between the religious demand for obedience and the personal claim of self-will. But we may also say that this demand for obedience is the promise of fulfillment. Obedience to God is really release from the frustration and emptiness of self-will. Obedience is fulfillment, release into what God has intended us to be. Let us look more closely at this claim.

Most of us are willing to admit that if God exists, we owe him our obedience. This just goes with being God—and man. If we can come to any assurance as to what he commands, we recognize his right to expect our obedience. We may dodge this responsibility by many clever devices. But I suspect most of us know, deep within ourselves, that we owe God our very being and therefore also our obedience.

We may cheapen our religion so that it becomes a way of getting God to bless what we want to do. But we really lose all respect for such a God and are dimly aware that such a religion is phony.

We know that there is a rightness about the simple

demand of Jesus: "If ye love me, keep my commandments" (John 14:15 KJV). This is proper and we know it. We may talk sentimentally about the gentleness and kindness of Jesus. But we know very well that there is a firm integrity about him. He demands that, if we are to take him seriously, we must obey him. And we know that this is exactly right.

However, there are two further aspects of this demand which we ought to recognize.

God's demand for obedience is also his promise of fulfillment. The reasonableness of this can be stated very simply. God is our Creator. He who has made us knows what is good for us. He wills only our good. Therefore, what he commands is really what we are intended to be. What he denies is only what is bad for us. What he demands is our way to fulfillment.

This is the reason why self-will is always frustrating. We are intended to be God's obedient children. In his will is not only our peace but our joy, our sole reason for being. And in discovering the reason for our existence we find the fulfillment of ourselves.

I remember an incident that occurred in one of our seminars in graduate school. We were seated around the table, talking intently. Suddenly our professor leaned forward and with a sparkle in his eye said, "Gentlemen, remember that sin can never be anything better than second nature!" We ought to remember this, or something like it, when we consider our own

53

willfulness, our tendency to want to do things our way. Our own way can never be anything better than second best, and that's not good enough. It is God's way which leads to fulfillment. It is only in his will that we find our true joy.

Just about now, if indeed not before this, the question will arise as to how we can know what is God's will. This is a real and troublesome question, but we need to be a little on guard against it. It can become an evasion. Endless debate about what is the will of God can be a way of avoiding serious commitment to that will. This is not to deny that the issue is a real one. We may argue earnestly and honestly about relativism, the variety of ethical teachings, rival claims to divine sanction. And such discussions may clarify what is God's will. But they may also provide a cover for our reluctance to surrender our wills. It requires honesty and humility, and perhaps a measure of divine grace, to know the difference.

The basic issue is whether you are willing to do God's will, regardless of what it is. Would you do it if you knew it? Which is to say, will you obey what you already know? You may not know everything about God's will for you, you may never know very much, but you know enough to get started. If you are truly willing to do God's will, and if you will obey what you already know, you will learn more about what he wants you to do. Knowledge of God's will comes only after the commitment to obey, only in the act of obedience. Jesus indicated this in a word addressed to a somewhat different but related issue: "If any man's will is to do his (God's) will, he shall know ... (John 7:17). Paul implied the same in one of his striking exhortations (Rom. 12:2): Do not be conformed to this world, but be transformed; let your mind be renewed ... then you will know what is the will of God.

We must not allow any uncertainty, real or imagined, concerning the specifics of the divine will, to distract us from our central will to obey. Obedience means fulfillment.

There is a further reason why obedience is the way of fulfillment. With the demand, God offers also the grace to obey. We learn this as we persevere in Christian experience, as we grow toward maturity.

Every one of us knows that obedience is not gained simply by being demanded. Obedience must be evoked. We parents have certainly learned this. It is not enough just to require obedience; we must strive to win free assent. Moreover, we quickly learn that to prohibit the wrong does not give any power to do the right. We learn this not so much from our children as from ourselves. We know what the prohibitions are. They warn us not to do certain things. But they provide no power at all to do any positive good. Surely, God has learned this. His commandments have been on record for a long time. And they are pretty consistently broken. We, his creatures, still have a hard time doing the kind of good we think he wants.

The wonder of the gospel is that God not only commands but offers grace to do what he commands. What is required is that our motives be changed. God offers to do this in the experience we know as conversion, the "turning around" of our lives, the turning from ourselves to God. What is required is that we be given a new kind of power. God offers this with the gift of his presence, his Spirit in and with us. What is required is that we shall mature in our capacity for obedience. And God offers this in his continuing presence, the inner working of his Spirit to guide and inspire our growth. This is the full promise of the gospel: what God requires he gives; with the demand for obedience he offers also the grace to obey.

Now I want to be realistic. There are many continuing moral battles we all have to fight. It is doubtless true that doing the will of God will always require discipline. There will always be a tension between some of our own desires and what we recognize to be the demand of God. But is there not also a sense in which doing the will of God becomes increasingly the thing we want to do, the thing we find it natural to do? I profoundly believe that it is possible for us to grow toward maturity, to increase in our capacity for glad obedience. This does not mean that our performance becomes faultless. But it means that we gain in understanding, in judgment, in self-management. And as we do, obedience to God becomes the natural expression of his working in us, and our own deepening sense of fulfillment in his will.

Just the other day I remembered something that happened during the war. I was coming home from Japan on a destroyer. Such a small ship was not used to carrying a chaplain, and they invited me to preach for them on Sunday morning. I remember saying something that some of my hearers did not quite believe, and it may not be altogether true. I tried to say that the will of God is not a straitjacket that forces us into an uncomfortable, unnatural position. The will of God is more like a comfortable jacket that is made especially for us, and that we wear year after year, until it begins to fit more and more easily.

The analogy may have its limitations. But it indicates one or two truths that we ought to keep in mind. The will of God really is tailor-made for us. It is made to fit, to enable us to move comfortably and easily in the way God intended. So the more we obey, the more we become what God intends us to be, and the more his will "fits." The more we yield to the grace and power which he gives, the more we find fulfillment in obedience.

So the word of Jesus which sounds like a command, also carries the accent of a promise, "If you love me, you will keep my commandments" (John 14:15). He said this in the context of the promise of the Holy Spirit. It is as if he were saying: Only love me. Learn to love me more than anything or anybody else in all your life. And you will keep my commandments. I will help you. My Spirit will dwell in you to give you guidance and insight and power. In this loving obedience you will find joy. And I will help you.

4

THE INSECURITY OF FEELING / THE ASSURANCE OF FORGIVENESS

"The Spirit helps us in our weakness."

The fullness of our faith may often be blocked by the fluctuations of our feelings. Sometimes what we take to be problems of faith may really be problems with our feelings. The relationship between feeling and faith is probably just as important as the relation between reason and faith.

UNMASKING OUR FEELINGS

We have been considering the hindrances to faith represented by pride and self-will and intellectual inquiry. Inevitably there has appeared the fact that these difficulties stir up feelings which interfere with our faith. So we have talked about guilt and anxiety and loneliness. These feelings get in the way of our faith. Perhaps now we should bring this fact out in the open and look at it more specifically.

There is an implicit danger here, of course—that of

reducing theology to psychology, of identifying religious experience and mental health, of defining all difficulties of faith as disturbances of feeling. But there is an opposite danger as well—that of reducing theology to intellectual aptitude, of supposing that religious experience can be quite independent of emotional stability, of failing to see that disturbed feelings may indeed disrupt faith.

Sometimes this occurs on relatively simple levels.

Not long ago I was fighting off a spring cold. There were a few days when I didn't feel at all well. And, of course, the more I thought about it, the worse I felt. I dragged myself through the day's work, not producing much, and not caring whether I did. There were times during those days when, if my faith had depended on my feelings, I would have had no faith worth talking about. Still I realized that the problem was not one of theology but of health. My faith was being interfered with by my feelings. But grappling with a minor illness is such a simple and normal experience that it really didn't disturb me very much. Most of us have learned to handle this kind of situation.

There are more serious dimensions to this instability of our feelings. In this day of popularized psychology, we have learned a good deal about the relation of parent and child and the consequent development of our self-understanding. So a question is frequently asked which may take the following form: "Is it possible for a person who has never really experienced love to believe that God loves him? That is, there are persons who, particularly in certain critical, formative periods of their lives, have not been loved, have been rejected. Is it possible for these persons really to grasp the meaning of divine love? Or to state it differently, if a person has had a poor, hateful relation with his own father, what happens to him when he is told that God is his heavenly father?"

Frankly, I believe there is no simple or easy answer to this question either way. It is clearly an instance in which our faith is closely related to our feelings. The undependability of our feelings may result in an apparent uncertainty of faith.

The more deeply I come to know people, and something of the secret agitations they carry around inside themselves, the more I am convinced that we are frequently prevented from enjoying the fullness of faith because of the instability of our feelings. We are ill at ease with ourselves, perhaps because of serious family problems, perhaps because of emotional confusions of long standing. Our faith is correspondingly unclear, insecure, unsatisfying, unrewarding. We don't really know why. But it is perfectly clear that no amount of intellectualizing about our faith seems to do much good. It is apparent to me that we must also understand our feelings—what they are, why they are as they are, how they affect us, and how to handle them. The intellectual, volitional, and emotional aspects of faith must be developed together, just as these three aspects

61

of our being—mind, will, and feeling—are inseparably bound together.

When talking with persons who seem to be caught in such circumstances, I try to illustrate the condition in this way. Our feelings and our faith both operate by means of the same equipment in our selves. The instruments or mechanisms of our personality which we use in faith are the same instruments or mechanisms through which our feelings operate. So that if our feelings are out of kilter, our faith is likely to be out of adjustment also. (Whether it also works the other way will have to be considered a little later.) When our capacity to love and understand is disturbed, our capacity for faith is shaken also. If our feelings are confused, our faith may seem to be insecure.

It is rather like the combination radio-television-phonograph which many of us have in our homes. If something goes wrong with one of the speakers, let us say, or with one of the connections in the sound system, all three of the operations are affected. A scratch on the cabinet might annoy us, but it would not affect the operation of the set itself. But if something goes wrong with a particular tube, or with a speaker, all three operations are distorted, because all three use the same mechanism.

The analogy may have serious limitations. A good electronics man might tell me it isn't even accurate. But it helps me to visualize what I think is true inside of us. Our feelings and our faith operate through the same personality structure, use the same mechanisms of the self. Therefore, they influence one another.

Moreover, our feelings are usually shaped before our faith is formed. So the influence is most frequently experienced in that direction—from feelings to faith. It is only much later in our personality development and religious growth that we can establish the reverse influence—from faith to feelings. At the moment, what we must understand is that emotional insecurity often feels like a threatened faith.

MANAGING OUR FEELINGS

We have already identified some of these deep feelings. They have become the everyday terms of popular psychology.

There is *anxiety,* an undefined fear, an uneasiness without discernible cause. There is *insecurity,* which may make us compensate in many aggressive, self-assertive ways. Often there is a deep and subtle *guilt,* which we may not recognize as such, but which makes it difficult for us to accept forgiveness.

Most of us have an assortment of *animosities* (the blunt word is hate). Many of us find it difficult to love. Our power to love is inhibited by alien feelings. We are frequently *afraid* of other people. We put up a protective front, and cannot open up to one another. Consequently, we experience *loneliness, alienation, estrangement.*

It seems perfectly accurate to say that most of us carry around inside ourselves most of these feelings, in some combination or other. They may have bothered us over a long period of time. Or specific events may stir them up and cause particular ones to disturb us. And added to these are the daily ups and downs, the fluctuations in feelings due to changes in body chemistry, or organic functions, or the weather, or family tensions, or any number of everyday factors. And until we arrive at some understanding of these emotions, both central and peripheral, faith may be hindered.

Mental health, as I understand it, means bringing these emotions into good working relations with the other functions of the self, intellect and will. And this is a point at which we have to think rather carefully.

There are some schools of psychology which assert that we are completely dominated by our deepest emotions. This is particularly characteristic of a certain type of post-Freudian popularization of psychology. The impression is conveyed that we are really driven by these deep, compulsive powers, and that there is little we can do about them in terms of intellect or will. But there are one or two subtle errors here which we need to see.

First of all, the understanding of our emotions cannot itself be an emotion. To understand ourselves, and these deep compulsive powers, requires the use of intellect. After all, the various schools of psychotherapy are highly intellectualized systems of theory and practice. Understanding them involves the gaining of insight, the use of reason, the exertion of will (if nothing else, the sheer hard work of mastering theory).

Moreover, even to say "I am dominated by my emotions" is an intellectual statement. One makes such a statement as an assertion of judgment. Admittedly, one does not really know the power of these deep drives until this knowledge is deeply felt. Admittedly, self-knowledge is emotional as well as intellectual, and the admission of certain aspects of self-knowledge frequently requires considerable courage of will. But it is simply inaccurate to say that we are completely dominated by our emotions, because the very assertion requires the use of intellect and will.

To be a healthy person, then, means to bring our feelings into a healthy working relation with all the aspects of the self. Wholeness of the person means the effective interrelation of all the powers of the self.

Similarly, wholeness of Christian experience means bringing all of these chaotic, half-understood feelings into a workable relationship with our faith. Faith and feelings play upon one another. They are not separable from one another. We must have sufficient understanding of both to have insight into their interrelationship, and sufficient purpose of will to bring both into effective interaction.

Our approach to this experience must be from both directions, and probably from both directions at once.

We cannot simply psychologize faith. And we cannot wholly intellectualize feeling. We must understand our feelings so we can manage them. And we must understand our beliefs so we can interpret reality, including ourselves. Then faith will become what it is intended to be, an act of the whole person, a commitment of one's self in loving obedience to God, a finding of one's self in harmony and trust.

In the life of the church I tend to approach Christian experience from the perspective of theology. I believe that Christian growth comes through study. Therefore, I emphasize the importance of serious inquiry into the meaning of the gospel. The need for this seems evident. Most contemporary Protestants simply do not know what the Christian faith is. Yet one of the first requisites to being a Christian is to know what it means to be a Christian. And the only way to learn this is to study: to study the primary sources, Scripture; to learn something about the Christian experience of others from Paul to our contemporaries.

Yet I know perfectly well that study is not sufficient by itself. Faith is not simply a matter of understanding with your head what the New Testament teaches or what contemporary theologians are saying. Indeed, the New Testament itself teaches us that this is not so. Faith is an act of the whole person, a total commitment of one's self to the God who gives himself to us in Jesus Christ. That is to say, faith involves our feelings.

The organic process which faith is, is a living experience in which the whole self is active.

Faith is a certain knowledge of ourselves, our relation to God and God's attitude to us. This knowledge must get into our feelings. We must feel ourselves forgiven as well as think ourselves forgiven. But our feelings do not readily submit to our intellect or our will. We do not simply command our feelings to line up and fall in place. So our feelings have to get into our knowledge too. We have to feel our way into faith. Knowledge of the gospel and knowledge of ourselves are both involved in the knowledge that we really are the forgiven children of God. And all three kinds of knowledge have to grow and develop together in authentic Christian experience.

Characteristically, I tend to approach all this from the point of view of theology. But I know very well that theological aptitude and correctness of belief are not nearly enough to make a person a Christian. Just as characteristically another minister or teacher may begin with the psychological analysis of feelings and the wholeness of emotional life. But good psychological adjustment does not exhaust the meaning of Christian experience. Personal growth must be grounded in a Christian understanding of ourselves and the meaning of our lives. This Christian understanding must be expressed in a growing realization of the self.

In mental health we try to understand and manage our feelings so that we may live effectively. In Christian experience we try to understand our feelings in the light of our faith, so that we may live as children of God.

MASTERING OUR FEELINGS

What are some of the practical ways by which we can master our feelings and make them allies of our faith?

First of all, we can affirm the love of God and his willingness to forgive us, regardless of our feelings. God loves us, whether or not we feel as if he does. He has gone to considerable trouble to convince us of his love. This is what the cross means. He truly wants to forgive us. And if we let him he will. This is true whether we feel like it or not. This is the objective affirmation of the gospel. Its truth does not depend on the condition of our liver, or on barometric pressure, or on family relations. The love of God is grounded in his own faithfulness. And we may affirm this regardless of our feelings. This is where Christian experience usually begins.

Our feelings may not even confirm our affirmation. Having claimed the love of God, we may not experience any particular response of feeling. Some people think they should feel different, or the religious experience is not dependable. But it is precisely our feelings that are not dependable. And if they are not particularly stirred by the affirmation of God's forgiving love, we should not be either surprised or disturbed. Their response is not really relevant.

The fault may be in the receiving set, not in the sending station. God is love. God does will to forgive you. He is sending this message loud and clear. But there is static in the air, or there is a faulty tube, or a loose connection. Or it may be that the set needs a thorough overhauling. In any case, the message is true. You may affirm it to be true. You may say, "I get the message," and never mind what your feelings say.

To affirm means also to accept the forgiving love of God. This will mean surrendering pride and self-will, to the extent that you are aware of these hindrances. And perhaps you may have to assume that proud self-will is present even though you are not particularly aware of it, and surrender, yield yourself to God. This is the other side of accepting the divine forgiveness. Your affirmation then would be, "I am forgiven. I accept God's loving forgiveness."

But some will ask, "How do I accept his forgiveness?" This question is often raised in all seriousness. How do I accept God's gift? And I must confess that the answer somewhat baffles me.

If I wanted to give you a present, how would you accept it? You would simply accept it! It seems to me that this is one of those basic words which almost defy definition, a basic act which can hardly be described. If I were to offer you a gift, and then spell out in detail just how you were to accept it, you would think me rather strange. Or if I were to offer a gift, and you were to stumble over definitions of acceptance, I would think you rather strange. I would simply offer it, you would simply accept it, with appropriate expressions of thanks and appreciation, and that is all I would expect.

Something like this must be true with respect to our acceptance of God's gift. He offers us love and forgiveness. He offers it with unimaginable proofs that he really means it. His love is a suffering love; it takes the shape of a cross. His forgiveness is a costly forgiveness; he gives himself in his Son. The first affirmation of our faith is the acceptance of his loving pardon.

Second, we must give this affirmation time to help us with our feelings. Perhaps a better way to say it is that we must allow God time to help us. We have made an affirmation. It may be primarily intellectual or volitional. Now we must let this affirmation sink deeply into our feelings.

A large part of Christian growth is precisely this matter of letting our faith work in and through our feelings. To be sure, growth in the Christian life means deepened understanding of beliefs. It means development of moral insight and social concern. But it also, and perhaps most deeply, means increasing mastery of our feelings.

This process of growth is what has been known in Christian doctrine as sanctification. It means letting God, by his Holy Spirit, work in us so that we may experience increasing maturity. It is my impression that this aspect of the Christian faith has been neglected in recent years, or else reduced to moral exhortation and psychological self-help. But the full range of the gospel must include the promise of growth. If we will let him, God will help us become better persons. He will help us grow toward maturity. He will help us achieve increasing self-understanding, mastery of our feelings, and direction of our powers toward his purposes.

There are several practical steps we may take in this exciting, rewarding experience of Christian growth.

First of all, we need the best possible psychological insight. We need to know ourselves as well as possible, and psychology is certainly a necessary ally at this point. It is, par excellence, the primary instrument of self-knowledge.

We must be somewhat careful at this point. There are many varieties of psychology, many schools of thought, many types of therapy. We must not allow ourselves to be deceived by oversimplified, popularized presentations of psychological self-help. But we certainly do need the best insight we can gain. This means study and inquiry. It means conversation and communication— perhaps through various types of small group experience. It means seeking out and laying hold of the best possible resources in this whole field of self-knowledge and self-management.

Second, however, and an immediate second, we must remember that Christian experience is not only a matter of psychological insight, but is also a matter of receiving the positive action of God. So that at the same time as we are seeking the best insights we can discover, we are seeking also to be receptive and open to the work of God in us. Remember that God is always on the initiative. We don't have to do everything by ourselves. Indeed, we can't do everything by ourselves. God is constantly and actively giving himself to us, guiding and sustaining our best efforts. We only need open ourselves to his working in us.

Paul makes an interesting statement in this respect (Rom. 8:26): "The Spirit helps us in our weakness; for we do not know how to pray as we ought, but the Spirit himself intercedes for us with sighs too deep for words." (I must confess a preference for the King James Version, "with groanings which cannot be uttered"; this speaks the agony, the heart-searching agony of self-knowledge.) For a long time I could not imagine what Paul meant by this. It impressed me as being profound, and I liked the sound of it, but I certainly did not know what it meant. Then one day it came to me that Paul's statement is actually related to a truth which is common knowledge to every counsellor.

When we sense ourselves to be disturbed by some problem, we frequently do not really know what the deepest cause is. We may suspect some things, but the real issue may lie much deeper. Or we may unknowingly cover up the deeper problem by looking around at the more obvious needs. In any case, self-knowledge requires that we get beneath the surface disturbances and get at the real problems that are disturbing us. This is not easy. It is usually painful. We tackle this particular bit of self-knowledge with great reluctance. And we may finally admit that we need the help of some counsellor.

Suppose that, as an average Christian, I am praying about my problems, all the while not knowing what my real problem is. I am asking God, sometimes in great earnestness, to help me with what I think are my problems. But because I don't really know what is deeply troubling me, I cannot pray intelligently or knowingly. In Paul's accurate phrase, I do not know how to pray as I ought.

But God will help you to know yourself, if you let him. Let your prayer be for God to show you what is really eating at you. Pray that he will search out your deepest needs and bring them to the level of your awareness. Open yourself to his probing. Expose yourself to his searching. Let him reveal to you, sometimes by way of psychological insight, sometimes by way of helpful counselling, sometimes by way of the mystery of private discovery, let him reveal to you what is deeply troubling you. Then you will know what to pray for, and he will be able to answer in a new dimension. In Paul's words, the Spirit himself intercedes for us with groanings which we don't know how to utter.

Third, as we increase in our understanding of ourselves, let us seek to be more understanding of others. As we become more aware of our own confused feelings, and the strange things they do to us, we should become more sensitive to others. We will realize that behavior is not always what it looks like on the surface. We will realize that there are deep feelings moving underneath the visible exteriors of our friends and associates, and we should be sensitive to their deepest needs. As this happens, our relations with others will be transformed. There will develop a mutual understanding and support which are a large part of what the New Testament calls love.

Fourth, we must be alert to the moral implications of our faith. If we really let God guide us, he may lead us into moral decisions which will be difficult. We may have to be purged of false ambitions and goals. We may have to reject some of the values and standards of our culture and commit ourselves to other aims.

We may as well level with ourselves at this point. If we are not willing to let our lives be changed where they need it, we had better not get mixed up with Christianity. We had better find some other religion— popular Protestantism, maybe. But in any case avoid serious Christian faith. Because if we commit ourselves to genuine faith, God will require that we be obedient to whatever he may demand.

This may or may not mean a serious change in your present way of living. There is no way to determine this in advance. It all depends on what you are doing now. Your present life may be characterized by such moral earnestness and straightforward thinking, that deepening Christian experience will not require any serious redirection. It will simply yield a greater sense of joy and fulfillment. On the other hand, it may be that there are some aspects of your present practice that will require alteration, perhaps radical overhauling. And you must be willing to face up to this possibility, or forget the whole business.

But if you have come this far, so far as to seek to open your life to the searching, strengthening presence of God, then hopefully you will not turn back from this moral demand. For there can be no deep healing of the emotions without an accompanying dedication of the will. And such obedience, rooted in faith, will result in continuous moral growth.

Then, in the fifth place, let us seek whatever opportunities of service and helpfulness we are fitted for in the community. We must not be driven to nervous activity—busyness—by our unresolved tensions or by our false grabbing after status. But the fullness of Christian experience does require that we not be concerned exclusively with ourselves but that we turn outward to others. This may mean working in some phase of church life. It may mean participating actively in some community group. It may mean helping to tackle a tough civic problem. In any case, the sort of self-understanding and personal growth we are talking about ought to eventuate in, and be strengthened by, some active service in the life of the church and community.

I think this is the sort of experience Paul is describing in some of the ethical sections of his letters. We must be careful not to make Paul into a twentieth-century psychologist. But we should be equally careful not to read him as if he were a nineteenth-century moralist. He was a first-century Christian. Too often we read him moralistically rather than psychologically, as if he were laying down demands for behavior rather than laying bare the dynamics of behavior.

I believe that his insights may be more truly understood if we realize that he is addressing himself not only to moral problems but also to emotional confusions.

Consider a passage in the third chapter of Colossians, for example; it could be paralleled by others. He writes that we should put away impurity, passion, evil desires, covetousness. We should try to get rid of anger, wrath, malice, slander. How? By being "raised with Christ," that is, accepting the renewing power which God can give us through our faithful acceptance of his love. Such a cleansing of troublesome emotions is not a moral exercise; it is the work of God in us. So this passage is not so much a moral exhortation as it is a plea to let God do his work with us. If we let him, he will give us compassion, kindness, lowliness, meekness, patience, forgiveness—all of them components of love.

Are you willing to do this? Are you willing to spend the rest of your life at this? It will probably take that long! But what else do you have to do that is as important and as rewarding as this?

Let God cleanse, transform, establish your feelings.

Then you will sense yourself increasingly established in the faith. Then you will respond with more and more gladness and gratification to Paul's final exhortation: "Whatever your task, work heartily, as serving the Lord and not men."

5

THE FAILURE OF THE CHURCH / THE CALL TO COMMUNITY

"You are the body of Christ."

One of the most impressive marks of the church is its failure. To say this in the midst of the obvious prosperity and success of the church may sound like nonsense. But every person who has any problems of faith will know exactly what I mean: the failure of the church to be the church is a serious hindrance to faith.

A FALTERING CHURCH

A very able churchman once took me to task for making such a statement. And he had a sound argument.

"How can you say the church is a failure?" he asked. "Look at the good it has accomplished in the community. Look at the solid leaders of business in our city. Look at the leaders in civic interests and concern for good government. Look at the people who are giving generously of time and work in the benevolent and service organizations of our city. Almost all of them are church people. I would say that the church has been quite successful in its influence on the life of our city."

He is right, of course. The churches have indeed motivated and encouraged men and women to live decently, to work sacrificially in community affairs. We all know that life in these United States is far from ideal. But we also know that there is a fund of solid decency, of dependable honesty, and of sincere good will upon which we all can draw in carrying on our daily affairs. And it is not an immodest claim to say that the churches have had a hand, a considerable hand, in shaping such a state of affairs. We must say this hesitantly, without self-satisfaction, and with awareness of frequent exceptions. But certainly some tribute may be paid to the sturdy and dependable moral strength which the churches have inculcated in many of their people, and on which the life of our communities seriously depends.

In fact, another man points out with great firmness that many of the benevolent enterprises of the community had their origins in the churches. Hospitals, relief for the needy, care of the aged and handicapped, organizations for the moral training of youth—many such services have begun in churches, or under the leadership of church people, growing out of Christian concern.

The same person will sputter with indignation that so many of these benevolent activities are "getting

79

away from the church." I try to reply in terms of the requirements of a pluralistic society, and dimensions of need that are beyond the resources of the churches. But he still makes his point, and well. The churches have injected many values and strengths into our common life.

Yet some of us cannot escape the haunting sense that the church has failed, and not just failure that you can admit with a shrug of the shoulders, but failure of the most desperate sort. Failure of the sort that is sensed by every troubled seeker after faith. Failure that is pointed out by every casual skeptic. Failure that seems to reflect discredit upon the faith the churches affirm. One of the most eloquent arguments against Christianity is the church.

We know this to be true. Yet when we stop and think about it, it is not immediately apparent why it should be true. After all, failure is not the exclusive prerogative of the church by any means. Just about every social institution, every organization that involves people is marked by the same kinds of failure that characterize the church. Indeed, one may say that the higher the stated purpose of the institution, the more likely it is to fall short of its aims.

Who ever heard of a perfect marriage? Successful marriages, yes—most of them achieved not without effort and agony. Some skeptics, therefore, may scoff at the married estate. But most people still seek in marriage a joy and fulfillment which no other human relation affords, and many find it.

Democracy is great. Few of us would really want to live under any other system. Yet we would be hopelessly sentimental, and dangerously naive, if we failed to recognize that American democracy is riddled with all the assorted deceits of politics. Any skeptic can point out the failures. But how many will trade it for another system?

Our economic order is basically sound. Most of us never had it so good. Yet we know, to our dismay, that in the midst of affluence there are appalling pockets of poverty. We know that mixed with a general honesty there is a treacherous amount of chicanery and double-dealing. But not many people are interested in rejecting the whole system.

This kind of failure seems to afflict every one of our social institutions. Yet for some reason, the failure of the church appears more damaging. I often wonder why.

Is it because the church claims so much for itself? The official doctrines of the church affirm that it is not simply a man-made institution but is of divine origin. Most church members do not bother with this doctrine. They accept the church at a much more prosaic, mundane level. But the church's understanding of itself is very exalted: God intends the church to exist; the church is the expression of the divine intention. Yet we have to admit that frequently the churches behave as if their point of origin were from quite the opposite direction.

Is it because we expect so much from the church? Even from the human point of view, it stands for some of the highest values in our civilization. The church champions the holiest teachings in our culture. And we expect it to reflect this holiness in its life. Yet an honest look at the contemporary church is frequently disheartening. Everybody knows that there are whole chapters of church history that might better never have been written. And supreme irony of all, these failures seem to have characterized the first-century church itself. Paul's letters to the Christians in Corinth are full of the most serious charges against the church in that city. The mildest is his complaint that "there is jealousy and strife among you." There was plenty else too.

As it was in the beginning, it is now. And, we groan, will it ever be? Realism replies, probably so. We humans being what we are, probably so.

Yet Paul's very criticism reveals the hope for the church. First of all, the church produces its own most serious critics. The most incisive judgments against the church are pronounced by those who know it best—from within—and love it most. Second, it was precisely this troublesome congregation in Corinth which elicited Paul's most eloquent hymn to love. The sting of our criticism of the church as it is grows out of the clarity of our vision of what it should and may be.

FORMING A COMMUNITY

It is the prophets within the church itself who see its real failure. Actually, none of the criticisms mentioned thus far gets to the root of the matter, which is not a moral but a religious failure. And even though there is a danger in dwelling too much on the negative, we must see what these deeper criticisms of the church are, so that we may see where the real recovery lies.

The basic weakness of the church, say its perceptive prophets, is its failure to be what God intends it to be. Its members hardly regard themselves as the "people of God." Most of them would mutter that they don't even know what the phrase means. They are content to consider themselves a valuable social institution, an organization that contributes to the well-being of the community. ("You wouldn't want to live in a community without one, would you?") Hardly recognizable as the "body of Christ," the church has become a big business, with enormous vested interests, whose administrators keep an anxious eye on all the measurable signs of success. ("How big is your budget? How many new members did you receive last year?") And many ministers are hard pressed organization men, intent on running a successful institution and program, whose sermons are designated to give their people a religious shot in the arm, and occasionally an ethical jab, wherever they need it most.

There may be elements of caricature in this swift portrayal. But the features are recognizable. Many laymen, and most ministers, know it with genuine agony.

There are exciting exceptions to the general picture. And these exist precisely where ministers and people are discovering what the church is really meant to be, and where its growing reality is bringing meaning and excitement into their lives.

What then is the church meant to be? And by "church" I mean the local congregation. It is here that the church actually has reality for its members. I have no quarrel with the ecumenical movement. But what really concerns me is what the church is in the lives of its members who live and work in a given locality.

The shape of the local church is meant to be a community. That is, the church is made up of men and women and youth who are bound together by ties deeper than the accident of living in the same neighborhood or town or city, deeper than the coincidence of belonging to the same congregation. Community requires some sense of being related to one another in ways that are out of the ordinary: in this instance, being drawn into the church not simply of one's own volition but also by the call of God; being committed to the same Lord and Savior; being united to one another in a bond called love; being engaged in common Christian tasks in the wider communities of business, neighborhood, city; being bound by similar concerns for the world and similar hopes for eternity.

In all honesty, we have to admit that no local church

is likely to become a single community. This is not simply a matter of numbers; it can be as true of a church of 250 as of a church of 2,500. A conventional congregation has to be of some minimum size in order to maintain its existence. And how many of these members can really know one another? Or, to put it bluntly, how many want to know all the other members? There are practical limitations on the number of people with whom we can become deeply involved.

So it would be more accurate to say that the local congregation is designed to become an aggregation of communities. A case could be made that God's intention for the church never involved anything like the modern large congregation. But this is what the church has become, and in varying forms what it has been for a long time. There probably is no return to the earliest, primitive communities of the first Christian generation. But surely we can hope for communities within our congregations. These would be groupings of people who are bound to one another by ties of varying sorts, but which include the ties of common faith, mutual affection, and concern for one another.

Those of us who live within the church know, gratefully, that such communities do exist, imperfectly, fragmentarily, but really. We see it when bereavement or other sorrow strikes a member, and the quick rallying of Christian friends gives support and courage to that person. We see it when a personal or family crisis threatens to shatter someone's life, until he feels the quiet acceptance and support of his friends in the church. We see it when young people are caught in bewildering consequences of unthinking folly, and then write to you later, saying how much the church meant to them while they were all mixed up. The community of Christ is frequently present in the church, often inarticulate, sometimes ill-formed, but there.

If the shape is community, there are three lines of relatedness that will give it more definite contour and more cohesive strength.

We are intended to be a community of faith: a community of men and women and youth who know what we believe, and even have some sense of why we believe, and whose lives are rather seriously based on that belief. We may not always be good at expressing these things, but the faith is there, and we are growing in it all the time.

After all, the church exists because of its faith. The church was formed because men and women had come to believe something about God and Christ and themselves, and they were irresistibly drawn together by the very terms of that faith. The church exists to nurture this faith in its members, to proclaim this faith to all who will hear, and to relate this faith to the workaday world. It is therefore essential that church members know what the faith is.

This requires study as well as worship. It probably requires study in small groups as well as in private or in the congregation. It requires study of the primary sources, the documents of Scripture. It requires the reading of serious books about the Bible, about Christian faith and experience. Too much Christian education stops with Sunday school, which is like concluding your general education in grammar school. And in a world which demands continuing study for almost everybody in any area of responsibility, the need for continuing Christian study should be self-evident.

But study is not enough, and genuine Christian inquiry never stops with mere book learning. Because what we learn in the Bible and in Christian conversation just happens to be the redeeming power of God. And when he takes hold of us, our study becomes an exciting life-directing experience.

A businessman speaks quietly but urgently of the sense of purpose which God has given to his life: "In our church we believe in God. We believe in Jesus Christ as God's Son and our Savior. We are engaged together in continuing search and growth. And out of this comes a sense of purpose for my whole life."

A young married woman says spiritedly, "I never knew Christian experience could be so exciting."

A young couple says, "Our experience in church has meant more to our marriage than anything else that ever happened to us."

A college student says, "God is the center of my life. Everything else—my morals, my interest in civil rights, my relation to my parents, what I want out of life— everything else has grown out of this fact."

A young man who had been floundering in his vocation, but has now found himself in the ministry, exclaims, "I've never had so much fun in my life."

This faith which gives direction to our lives will be the faith of the New Testament, the classic Christian faith, even though it may not be expressed in the conventional terms of previous generations. Such faith will find its center in God's act in Jesus Christ. It will affirm that here God reveals himself in a definitive manner, and here God acts redemptively on our behalf. But contemporary Christians will be seeking new and relevant ways to express this faith.

Such a faith must be much more sophisticated than the simple faith of previous generations. (This simplicity may be romanticized in retrospect. But such is the aura frequently cast over the good old days of unquestioning faith.) In our time, faith must be related to circumstances and complexities that our parents and grandparents never imagined. Men of sober scientific intent speak learnedly of the possibility of life on distant planets. What does this mean for the centrality of Christ? Profound psychological insight into the murky depths of human personality has become common knowledge. What does this mean for the possibility of conversion and real change of character? Communications and mobility throw us into contact with other cultures, other religions. What does this mean for Christian claims to truth? All media of communications and entertainment expose the youngest and tenderest of minds to strange and fearful emotions and drives, leading unprepared adolescents into adult confrontations. What does this mean for values and standards that have been conventionally accepted?

These issues cannot be postponed or ignored. Most of us are already in the thick of them. Certainly our student generation is. And the local congregation must be a community of faith in which the whole range of culture is related creatively and redemptively to our commitment to the God who comes to us in Jesus Christ.

The church is intended to be a community of action: a community of men and women and youth who are trying to act responsibly in the life of the larger communities of family, business, government, social, and civic affairs.

"Social action" in the conventional sense of the term means the concern which the church manifests in particular social issues, and the ways in which it implements this concern. Most denominations have official bodies through which they try to define positions, develop information, and influence the thought and action of the people of the churches. But we all know that such pronouncements and policies are often far from the life of the local church, and how frequently local churches in effect repudiate the position taken by the denomination. Such larger actions have their place. But what concerns us here is what happens in the local churches.

These churches too will have action groups which will try to bring the influence and power of the church to bear on social issues. They will support benevolent enterprises already functioning in the city and nation. They may even pioneer new services for their community. There will be committees concerned with racial issues and with legislation which has moral or religious implications. The cause of world peace and world government will be championed by similar groups. But it must be admitted that these actions do not involve significant numbers of the members. And only occasionally can any given church express itself with anything approaching a consensus.

There is another meaning to Christian action which is just as important as the conventional sense of the term. This is the sort of action which Christians carry on every day in their daily work, in their families, in their service to the schools, local government, civic enterprises, political organizations. And a local church should be a community of men and women who are knowingly engaged in the tension-filled task of trying to act responsibly, in a Christian fashion, in their everyday tasks. The sense of community in such engagement is very important. We should know that we are not alone in our tasks, that there are others similarly involved. We should thus strengthen one another, learn from one another, and most of all sustain one another in our Christian work.

The key word here is "vocation." We Christians should have a sense that we are called to serve God in our daily work. All Christians are in this kind of ministry. It is not only clergymen who are called to their work. But every Christian man and woman and young person is called by God to do his work—God's work—in the world. And we are not doing this alone. There are many of us, and we are strengthened by the knowledge that we are bound together in a community in which we can support and sustain one another.

One day I was having lunch with one of the most respected men in the church and community, a man of unquestioned integrity in business, and unlimited concern in civic affairs. As we talked about religious matters, he said, "Chet, I wish I could put God at the center of my life. I try. My wife and I have devotions in the morning. But I spend the whole day wrestling with problems of personnel, finance, property. And by the time I get home at night, I'm exhausted. I have no energy left for study or self-improvement. I wish I could put God at the center of my life."

"Wait a minute," I said.

"If you are trying, under God, to build a sound and honest business enterprise . . . if, under God, you are trying to make our city a better place in which to live and work . . . then you *are* putting God at the center of your life. This is your vocation, to serve God in your daily work. And what you do here in the Loop is every bit as much God's work as what I do in the church. In fact, it may even be more important in the long run. Our work in the church is to strengthen and motivate you, and maybe even offer some guidance, for your work in the world. And this is God's work. You *are* putting God at the center of your life."

And so with every Christian who is working responsibly in the larger circles of the neighborhood and city. The life of the family—how shall we measure the importance of that ministry? Some will enter politics and work for what they believe to be right in that realm. Others will serve on school boards, commissions on human rights, and similar agencies. Others will be involved in various volunteer services. Others will be concerned for cultural and artistic activities in the community.

All of us can know that we are doing God's work. And we can be bound together in a community of action, in which we sharpen our understanding of our daily tasks, deepen our motivation, enrich our resources of power, and strengthen one another in the work that will never be finished.

The church is intended to be a community of love: a community of men and women and youth who are really concerned for one another, are sensitive to one another, and able to minister to one another in the ways of love. This common concern is rooted in and grows out of our common commitment to God through Christ. We love one another because we know we are loved by him. We are able to love one another because his love has evoked and empowered our capacity to love.

Again, it is only realistic to recognize that the depth and strength of this relationship will vary among persons in any congregation. There will be small groups, intimate associations of varying kinds in the church, in which our relations will be closer, our sensitivity deeper, our sharing more intimate. There is a limit to which one can extend these relations. But there is no limit to the range of our honest concern for one another, our sensitivity to their feelings and needs, our openness to give compassion and understanding when they are needed. And this is what should happen in our churches.

Christians will disagree with one another about many issues, even in the life of the church. But can't we disagree and still love one another? Still respect one another's judgment, even where we differ? Still care for one another and seek the good of each, even if we don't see eye to eye in some matters? I think we can —indeed, we must. The greatest failure of the church is at this point. And at this point we could make our most effective witness. "See how these Christians love one another!" What was once an expression of admiration has become an exclamation of disgust. Let it become once again a word of wonder.

One church advertised for years "a welcome to persons of all races." The outside community was skeptical. Then came an opportunity for this claim to be implemented, and it was. Not without agony of decision and heart searching. But it was implemented.

Not everyone in the congregation has entered heartily into this community of love. But all who have been deeply touched by it have been genuinely blessed. They are better persons because of the richness of Christian love. Segments of the community outside, both secular and religious, remain skeptical. Some even seem to hope that this experience of Christian community might fail. But it has not. Indeed, it has grown in its depth and meaning to those involved. There is no denying the genuine community of love that is experienced there.

Paul had a word for it, as we might expect. He was writing to the Galatians, a far from untroubled community. He suggested that as far as Christians are concerned, what really matters is not how well we perform our religious practices. What really matters is that we discover a "faith which worketh by love" (Gal. 5:6 KJV) Paul may have intended this comment for individual Christians, but I think it may be applied to the community as well. What really matters is that we become a community of faith which works through love.

This divine call to community corresponds to our own deepest cry for community. We need to be related to others in these profound ways. We cannot be effective Christians in isolation from one another. We can live well as Christians only as we are nurtured and sustained in a community of Christians.

A community of faith—a common faith in God's unchanging love, everlastingly given to us in Christ, by which our lives are shaped and directed.

A community of faith which works—a common commitment which drives us out into the wider affairs of the world, motivating us to participate responsibly in the world's life.

A community of faith which works by love—a common concern for one another, sharing one another's joys, standing by in adversity, sustaining one another in compassionate service to the world.

6

THE MYSTERY OF SUFFERING /
WOUNDS THAT HEAL WOUNDS

"In the world you have tribulation."

One of the most serious hindrances to faith is the simple but inescapable fact of human suffering. I shall never forget the cute little Japanese girl in Tokyo who asked me, a representative of a different faith, the question which knows no religious or racial boundaries. "If there is a God, why is there so much suffering in the world? Especially, why do the innocent suffer?" Her look and accent were exactly those of hundreds of students on American campuses who have asked the same question. The unanswered doubt in her voice was exactly that of countless loyal believers whose faith is threatened by the same question.

This barrier to faith seems never to have been more formidable than in our time. Men of philosophy are even using this argument to buttress their doubts. It would be safe to guess that seldom before in the history of the West have so many men seriously challenged religious faith on the grounds of the depth and extent of human suffering.

Why should this be true in our age more than in any other?

One possible reason is encouraging. We have learned, in our time, through the advances of medicine and other sciences, that much suffering can be eliminated or at least eased. There is considerable public pressure upon all of us to help underwrite the research necessary to extend this knowledge. The alleviation of suffering is a highly valued humanitarian goal of our time. And we are hurt to see so many persons suffering needlessly from ills which could be corrected, or because they lack correctives already available. A decent feeling of sympathy for humanity may be one reason why we are so sensitive to this problem.

The other possible reason is quite different. It is the sheer weight of suffering which men have inflicted upon each other in recent generations. Ours has probably been the most destructive half-century in the history of mankind—with promise of still more unimaginable disaster. In two successive wars and assorted forays, with the development of weapons of enormous destructive power, we have succeeded in wiping out millions of lives, inflicting continued suffering on countless others, and the end is not yet in sight. Many sensitive minds of our century are deeply hurt by the overwhelming weight of this suffering inflicted upon men by other men.

On the one hand, we can become impervious to this destructiveness. Note the automobile, one of the most murderous machines ever invented, but no one proposes to ban it. On the other hand, we are deeply wounded by our cruelty. We can't quite keep from wincing at the hurt of others. And already the question is implicit. Why?

A FAITH THAT IS HURT

It is not immediately apparent why the fact of suffering should constitute a barrier to faith. Yet we know very well that it is so. And at no point in our experience is the close connection between emotion and intellect more clearly visible.

Suffering hits us where it hurts. It hits us in our feelings. Our immediate response is emotional. The "Why?" that is wrung from our lips is not an intellectual question at all. It is a cry of anguish, forced from us by our suffering or the suffering of others. Yet this profoundly emotional reaction frequently turns into an apparently intellectual challenge to faith.

Why is this so?

The reason seems to be that almost automatically we pin the responsibility for suffering on God—if there is a God. How much this is due to the way most of us are brought up, and how much is due to something pretty deeply a part of our makeup, I am not sure. The fact seems to be that we almost inevitably assume that if there is a deity, he is somehow responsible for the circumstances of suffering. The assumption runs like this.

If God is, he must be responsible for everything that exists. Suffering exists, and is an awful thing that should be wiped out. But God (if he exists) does not wipe it out. He allows anguish to continue. Such a God is unworthy of our worship. We refuse to believe in such a deity.

This argument is only strengthened by certain over-strained statements of faith which underscore the insistence that God is indeed responsible for suffering. Such faith goes on to assert that, although it is hard for us to understand, God will work it all out in his own good time. He may inflict hurt on us. But it is part of his plan. And it will prove to be for our good.

However, the troubled seeker is unimpressed by this argument. Adequate faith is still challenged by an argument that emerges out of a hurt we all feel at one time or other.

There are several possible positions which troubled men may take with respect to suffering.

One sort of stoic humanism is expressed in Thomas Hardy's *Tess of the D'Urbervilles,* and most graphically in a famous sentence which introduces the last paragraph in that novel. Tess, the protagonist, has suffered a life of misfortune and tragedy. As a final indignity she is executed by the state as a criminal. In the closing scene we, the readers, are standing on a hill overlooking the prison where Tess is to be put to death. Eventually the flag is raised, telling us that she has been executed. The author comments, "'Justice' was done, and the President of the Immortals . . . had ended his sport with Tess."

Actually, Hardy did not really believe in any such deity. He couldn't. He had too much regard for humanity to believe in a God who could put a human being through such agony just for the "sport" of it. He was simply giving a cruelly ironic twist to his unbelief. He was caught in his own logic: if there is a deity, he must be responsible for the unjust order of things which had tortured Tess. Apparently, there was no Christian to suggest a more humane, biblical alternative. So Hardy, unable to accept such a God, rejected the only form of Christian faith he had known. And he was left with only his sad stoicism.

Mark Twain is regarded as a great humorist, and, of course, he was. But he was also an anguished man who had lost his faith. He expressed his loss in *Letters from the Earth*. This is an impassioned, fretful outcry against the suffering inflicted upon humanity, and against a God who would allow such conditions to continue. It is, at last, a rejection of faith because of the unsolved mystery of "Disaster, Disease, and the rest."

Twain bitterly portrays the fly and the microbe as the dread carriers of disease. And precisely these are the favorite creatures of the Creator. Yet man, foolish man, especially foolish Christian man, "having thus made the

Creator responsible for all those pains and diseases and miseries above enumerated, and which he could have prevented, the gifted Christian blandly calls him our Father!" (Note that according to Twain's understanding, Christianity makes the Creator directly responsible for all miseries, in spite of the fact that he could prevent them if he would.)

Obviously the man who writes this is hurting. He is hurting bad. Those who know his biography can guess what caused the hurt. Mark Twain is writing out of his personal agony. This agony becomes the bitter rejection of the only kind of Christianity he knows.

Archibald MacLeish has dealt seriously with the problem of suffering in his poetic drama, *J.B.* It is his retelling of the biblical story of Job, but it is recounted against the background of an age of unbelief, in which biblical faith no longer prevails. This is discernible in the very names of the principal characters: Nickles, the demonic figure, is a little less than the old Nick; Zuss, the deity, is not quite Zeus; and J.B. is something less than Job.

The sufferings of J.B. are overwhelming. And in the midst of his agony he cries out for all of us:

> What I can't bear is the blindness,
> Meaninglessness—the numb blow
> Fallen in the stumbling night.

And Nickles, devilish fellow, sings the timeless taunt of unfaith:

If God is God He is not good,
If God is good He is not God.

The only faith which MacLeish can offer is a humanism just a shade removed from the stoicism of Hardy. At the end of the play, J.B.'s wife concludes, "Blow on the coal of the heart." Find in the warmth of human affection the courage to endure. It may be that, apart from Christian faith, this is the most we can say. It is admirable to say so much. But is it enough?

A FAITH THAT HEALS

In trying to interpret the experience of suffering, I should like to mention a distinction which has been very helpful to me. It is the distinction between "problem" and "mystery." A "problem" is an issue which is outside me, so to speak, a matter over against which I can stand, and to which I can discover a "solution." A "mystery" is an issue in which I am personally involved, from which I cannot really disentangle myself, and to which I can find no objective solution but only a living resolution. I cannot solve a mystery; I can only resolve to live it. Therefore there is no "solution" to the "problem" of suffering. There is rather a comprehension of the mystery of suffering.

So if I speak of the "problem of suffering," it is merely a manner of speaking for the sake of simplicity. Suffering is not a problem; it is a mystery. This does not mean that there is little we can know about it or nothing we can do about it. It means simply that there is no complete answer to all the questions we can raise. Rather there is a way of living out the answers to the questions in which we are involved. If you ask why we suffer, you will find no answer. If you ask how we may suffer triumphantly, you will find an answer. And the answer is one of the most profound and pertinent insights of the Christian faith.

In each of the instances cited from the work of sensitive artists, the heart of the problem is seen to be the relation of God to our human condition. Each author, like most of us, draws a causal connection between God and our anguish. We make God responsible for our suffering. Therefore, we can never see God in any really helpful relation to our problem. And then we are forced to reject the only version of the faith we have heard, because that too seems to make God responsible for our condition.

It is exactly at this point that I want to deal with this issue. It is precisely the causal connection between God and our suffering that I want to sever. And the instrument which cuts through our common misunderstanding is the cross of Christ.

What I should like to say to men such as Hardy, Twain, and MacLeish—and to all such troubled persons —is this. If you want to understand the relation of God to our suffering, you must begin at quite another point. You must begin at the cross of Christ. If you take seriously the claim of the cross, you are confronted by a striking affirmation. God himself suffers. This is the first fact to be considered when pondering our own suffering. Suffering is not just a human experience. Suffering is part of the experience of God. We can no longer speak as if God inflicts suffering upon mankind. He himself is involved in it. We can no longer think of suffering as punishment with which God cruelly disciplines his creatures. He himself suffers.

Of course, this means taking seriously the Christian claim concerning Jesus Christ: that in some way which may forever elude our exact expression, "God was in Christ." If Jesus was just another "good guy" who in a manner contrary to popular stories was defeated by the "bad guys," then his death is just another illustration of the absurdity of existence. That such a man should be put to death in such a manner is absurd. And we are left closed up in the anguish of our meaningless agonies, relieved only by infrequent pleasures and indulgences.

But the Christian faith, taken seriously, can never settle for such an understanding of the cross. Instead we make the almost incredible assertion that God has really entered history in Jesus the Christ. However we may strain at words and stretch their meanings to express this faith, we truly and deeply believe that in the man whom we know as Jesus of Nazareth, God is expressing himself, disclosing his character and purpose, doing in history what we historical creatures cannot do for ourselves. And if this is true, then profoundly speaking, what happens to Jesus Christ happens to God. This death is not just a good man dying for what he believes. This death is the historical expression of the agony of God. The cross is a sign erected in history of what is eternally true in the life of God.

Moreover, God suffers deliberately. He does this in order to accomplish his divine purpose. He does it because he has to. It is his way of accomplishing what he most deeply wills—the truest joy of his funny, beloved little creature, man. Once we see this, we can no longer ask why does God make us suffer. He doesn't. He himself suffers too. So it is absurd to imagine that we should be exempt. Suffering is part of the very life of God. We can well expect that it will be part of our life as well.

We may still ask why, only this time on a much deeper level. Why does God suffer? He suffers because he loves his creatures, and in order to accomplish his loving will for them. It is of the nature of love to give one's self for the sake of the beloved. Could this be true on the human level if it were not already true on the divine level? To say that God is love is to affirm that God gives himself to and for his needy creatures. This self-giving is costly. God's love is suffering love. He gives himself in order to rescue us from our bewildering and tragic condition.

This is to take the cross with utter seriousness, not simply as an event in history, but also as an image of what is eternally true in the life of God. The passion and death of Christ mean that God embraces in his own self the whole range of human agony. Indeed, because he is God, his suffering is infinite, incomprehensible to us humans. We can only sense what that means as we see a man dying on a cross. And we know this is for us. We are involved in this death.

The religious etchings and paintings of Georges Rouault catch the depth of the divine suffering more profoundly than any others I know. In them we see the agony of man; but it is our agony caught up in the agony of God. And this divine agony is the ground of our hope.

It is precisely by his suffering that God achieves his purpose for his creation. The crucifixion issues in the resurrection. Both constitute one act of God. In the death of Christ God gains victory over all that would defile and destroy the life of man. He is victor, at infinite cost, over all that causes us anguish and despair. In this is our hope. In this is our victory.

Some time ago I heard a preacher on the radio tell a story, the error of which is relevant here. A great actor of a previous generation was asked what words in English literature he thought most beautiful. He replied, "Nobody knows the trouble I've seen. Glory, Hallelujah!"

The preacher went on to enlarge on this judgment. I kept waiting for him to point out the incomplete quotation. He never did. I still don't understand how any preacher could fail to see that the words that are omitted are precisely the crucial words. What the Negro spiritual really says is this:

> Nobody knows the trouble I've seen,
> *Nobody knows but Jesus!*

And it is exactly because Jesus knows, that is to say, God knows, that the Christian may say, "Glory, Hallelujah!" Most of us will never be uninhibited enough to say this out loud. But because we know that God knows, and cares, and can do something about it, we know a quiet joy even in the midst of trouble.

"But," you are bound to ask, "if God doesn't 'cause' suffering, how does it happen? Certainly we must suppose that he 'permits' it."

This is one way to say it. And we may allow such a form of words. Personally, I should prefer to be much more blunt and simply say God cannot prevent certain damaging, irregular events from happening. This may be too radical, and may not even be true. But in any case, and by some means of expression, we must recognize that God does limit himself to certain conditions which are essential to life, and which may cause suffering.

The regularity and dependability of the universe seem to be necessary to the emergence and continuance of life as we know it. There have to be some things we can count on: the sun coming up; the seasons changing;

107

the thrust and pull of forces. Sometimes these forces collide, as when two cars crash, or a storm is brewed. And suffering ensues. Or a group of cells go berserk and become cancerous. Or a body wears out and just gives up. Or a baby is born malformed. And there is suffering.

In these instances, God certainly does not cause the suffering. He does not cause the events which involve suffering. But he cannot, or will not, interrupt the necessary functioning of the universe.

God gives us freedom—and we abuse it. We eat too much or drink and smoke too much—then wonder why we get sick. We develop tensions in business, in cities, in homes—and wonder why we crack up. We drive cars too fast. We can't get along in the family of nations, not even in our own neighborhoods.

Certainly, God does not cause all the sufferings that are attendant upon these ills. But neither does he deny us the freedom in which these misfortunes are rooted.

What then can God do? He can help us grasp these misfortunes, overcoming some and making the most of others. He can help us use these circumstances for our best good and for the blessing of others.

This is what God does with his own suffering.

Such is the unique claim of the Christian faith: the suffering of God is the means by which he triumphs over evil and achieves his purpose for good. This claim becomes the clue to our own creative and redemptive use of suffering: as God fulfills his purpose not in spite of but through suffering, so may we achieve his purpose for us through our suffering. In some mysterious manner which is beyond our exact expression, it is necessary for God eternally to bear a cross, in order that he may give us the fulfillment that he wills for us. Just so it may be true, if we are his, that the suffering and hurt and anguish of our life may be caught up into his purpose and used for our good.

The practical question then is not why must I suffer. It is rather how does God want me to use this suffering. How can I make the most of it? It is not that God causes such and such a suffering to befall me, in order that I may learn from it or grow by means of it. But rather, in everything that happens he can help me learn something or grow from it. It is not that he makes it happen. Rather when it happens, he wants to help me make the most of it.

This is what Paul meant when he wrote, "We know that in everything God works for good with those who love him, who are called according to his purpose" (Rom. 8:28). Personally, I prefer this translation to the more familiar King James, which reads, "all things work together for good...." The new translation avoids the dangerous impersonalism of the old, which suggests that all events and accidents somehow work together for good. This easily becomes a pious determinism or fatalism. The new translation puts the emphasis where it belongs—on the One who works: "In everything God works...."

109

It must be noted that this promise is conditional. We have a tendency to slip into a pious mood when struck by misfortune, and claim unctuously that "all things work for good." Well, this just isn't so. And this promise is not intended for everybody. It is for "those who love him"; for those "who are called according to his purpose." And this is not a matter of tit for tat, or a nice reward for those who are good. It is a matter of simple common sense.

It stands to reason that God is able to do some things for those who have placed their lives in his care that he cannot do for those who live their own way. It seems perfectly clear that God can work with the person whose life is committed to the divine will in a way that he cannot work with the person who is bent on doing as he pleases. If we turn to God only when we are in a jam, there really isn't much he can do, and let's face it. But if our lives are in his hands, open to his direction, if we really want to be his persons, then he can take the worst that can happen to us and help us make something creative and good out of it.

This then is the way not only to understand but to make use of your suffering. Love God above all else. Let your way be committed to his purposes. Let your life be directed, your practices determined, by his will as best you can understand it. In good fortune and bad fortune, you are his person. Then, if misfortune strikes, don't panic. Ask God how to get through this difficult event, how to make best use of what may look like tragedy, what his will is for you in the midst of trouble.

On the same night that he was betrayed, Jesus—according to the author of the Fourth Gospel—talked long and quietly with his disciples. Among the many reassuring words he spoke were these: "In the world you have tribulation." It almost sounds like a promise. You can count on it. You will have trouble. "But be of good cheer," he continued, "I have overcome the world" (John 16:33).

Jesus said this before the agony of Gethsemane. He said it before the humiliation of his trial, the pain and disgrace of his public execution. He said it before the deepest agony of his utter loneliness on the cross.

"I have overcome the world." Perhaps he was saying, it is only by going through all of this that I can overcome the world for you. It is only by my suffering and death upon the cross, only by descending into hell and emerging from death, that I can overcome the world. And if you love me, if you yield yourself to my purposes, you will share my suffering but you will also share my victory.

Paul must have discovered something like this. The way I have it figured, he wrote, the sufferings of this present life are simply not worth comparing with the glory which will be revealed in us. For the whole creation—though it is frustrated by our falling away from God's purposes—the whole creation is groaning as if in travail to bring forth its fulfillment. And we share in this creative, redemptive anguish. So that, as the divine suffering is the price paid for our very lives, so our lesser suffering may be caught up in the purpose of God for our redemption, and indeed the redemption of the whole creation. This is the hope that gives meaning to our existence (Rom. 8:18-25).

7

THE THREAT TO MEANING /
THE DEATH OF DEATH

"Because I live, you will live also."

Death stands at the end of our existence like a great grey question mark. It throws a long shadow back over our days, and we live in this shadow. We try to dispel it by living hard. We may even try to make believe it isn't there. But in moments of painful shock or perceptive insight or occasional sympathy we are reminded that it is still there—the final enigma, the unresolved question, the haunting mystery.

Obviously, death comes under many guises. At the end of a long, fruitful life death comes with quiet and easy naturalness. After long suffering, when the body is weak and weary, death comes as a release. But just as often—perhaps more often—death comes shockingly, even crudely. The sharp crack of a mad assassin's rifle. The screaming crunch of cars. The flaming plunge of a plane. Or just as agonizingly the malevolent erosion of cancer, the sudden seizure of the heart, the sedated sleeping away of an incurable disease.

Frankly, most of us prefer not to think about it. We try to erase the whole question and smooth out the smudge such erasures usually make. We dismiss the whole business, and figure it will take care of itself when the time comes.

But there is psychological evidence that we don't really get away with it. Instead of putting the subject out of our minds, we shove it into the back of our minds, where it rankles and hurts without our realizing it. We are driven to live more intensely by this vague uneasiness about death, but it won't go away. The first thing we must do is face up seriously to the fact of death as a threat to any possible meaning to our existence.

ASSENT TO DEATH

There are two common attitudes toward death, either one of which may become a barrier to any adequate faith.

The first of these is what we may call the rational view, and it has two variations, the stoic and the existentialist. Both agree that death is the natural conclusion to our biological existence. It's the end. Period. There's no need to expect anything beyond it. Man is an animal, and he comes to the same end as all the rest of the animals. Let's make the most of what we have, the present. So the stoic.

This apparently rational point of view has considerable merit. It is courageous. It can be the basis for a useful and even distinguished life. But when you look at it a little more closely, it isn't quite so strictly rational as it appears.

In the first place, man cannot die like the rest of the animals, because man does not live like the rest of the animals. Among other things, man is the animal who must find some meaning and purpose for his existence. He is always asking what things mean, including his own life. So far as we know, the other animals are not particularly disturbed by this question. But we are. And because we are concerned with the meaning of life, we must also be concerned to discover whether there is any meaning to death.

Moreover, unlike the rest of the animals, man knows he is going to die. Again, we have no evidence that the other animals are especially bothered about this. But man—whether primitive or sophisticated—anticipates his death. We know that we are headed for death. As a matter of fact, when we are quite honest with ourselves, we know that we are living toward death from the moment of birth. If we stop and think about it, we recognize that the processes of death as well as the processes of life are at work inside every one of us at this very moment. This is a fact of life.

So it isn't quite "rational" to say that we should simply accept death as a natural fact which we share with all living creatures. We are different. And we should take the measure of that difference.

Another variation of the stoic view is the existentialist, which is widely accepted in our time. Death is indeed the end, says the existentialist. But it certainly plays havoc with life. Death is the final absurdity. The only meaning our lives can have is the meaning we give to them. This indeed is quite worth the effort. But let's not imagine it will make any difference in our destiny. Death is real. Death is earnest. And the grave is its goal.

Again one must admire the courage, forthrightness, honesty, and impatience with sham which characterize this view at its best.

Another way of regarding death is the exact opposite of the rational view, although it claims a rational grounding as well. It is the philosophical or religious view that man is indeed destined to die physically, but there is something about him which will survive death. Man is endowed with immortality. He has an immortal soul—call it what you will—which, through the experience of physical death, will emerge into eternal life.

The rationalist is likely to call this view illusory, wishful thinking. But the fact remains that man is the sort of creature who can create this "illusion." It is an open question whether he creates this out of nothing or out of some profound intuition of the truth. And a man may argue very persuasively that the intimation of immortality is not wishful thinking but a reflection of reality. Man dreams of immortality because the hope is deeply planted in his very nature. And the hope that is there corresponds to the deepest truth in the universe which produced him. This argument may sound old fashioned to the person initiated in contemporary thought, but it cannot be lightly dismissed.

In any case, many men refuse to admit that man will really die. Death is the illusion, they insist. Man has an immortal soul; or if you don't like that language, man is an immortal self who is destined for a higher experience beyond the present life. This is the traditional philosophical and religious understanding of man. It has a long and respectable history in philosophy and is almost universal in religion.

Admittedly, belief in immortality may take many naive and sentimental forms, and often does. So we speak softly of death as sleep, or transition, or "sailing over the horizon." We say sweetly, "There is no death."

The skeptic sputters, "Nonsense!" And he is right. But he is not justified in classifying all belief in immortality with such sentimentalities. It must be agreed that from the Greeks to the present there is a long, respected tradition of philosophy which affirms the possibility of immortality. Similarly, there is a venerable and almost universal religious tradition from the Hindus, and even from the primitives, to the present, in which the expectation of immortality is cherished.

These are the two serious views of death, philosophically and religiously grounded. That death is the end. And that death is not the end. Both views can be aids or threats to authentic Christian belief.

AFFIRMATION OF LIFE

Interestingly enough, the New Testament understanding of death is a little bit like both of these views in some respects, and quite unlike them in others. It is related to both but sharply critical of each. How does this happen?

In any comparison of various religions and philosophies, similarities appear. Frequently, thoughtful persons will conclude from this that the uniqueness of Christianity is compromised. Because there is a similarity in some basic convictions, they argue, the New Testament is merely another expression of a generalized sort of religion which is universal.

But there is another way of interpreting this relationship. If ultimate truth really resembles what is disclosed to us in the New Testament, we can expect that hints and glimpses of this truth should have been gained by wise men and seers and visionaries in other religions. For instance, if it is true that God, from all eternity, intends to reveal himself definitively in history as a man among men, is it not reasonable to suppose that seers of many faiths should have had intuitions of this truth, which they expressed in their own partial fashions? The resemblances, then, between the New Testament claim and the claims of other religions may be a vindication of what is fully and finally revealed in Jesus Christ. And in interpreting the similarities, we must also pay close attention to the differences.

So in this matter of death. Men of varying faith, dispersed through time and space, have had glimpses of the truth concerning the meaning of death and the possibility of life after death. So it is not surprising that wise philosophy and honest religion resemble at many points the teachings of the New Testament. Neither is it surprising that New Testament faith must qualify or even reject aspects of these other views. The definitive truth about life and death is disclosed to us in the whole fact of Jesus Christ. His ministry, his crucifixion, and resurrection constitute the clue to our understanding of death and its meaning for life. The New Testament, then, makes two affirmations about death which are closely related to the two religious and philosophical interpretations we have just outlined.

Like the stoic and the existentialist, the New Testament regards death as utterly serious. Death is not simply something that happens to the body and leaves the soul untouched. Death happens to the whole person. Death may be the end, the end of everything for the person involved. Death is annihilation. Nothingness. Non-being. Just ask yourself, "What if I should no longer exist?" It is this possibility which the New Testament confronts quite honestly. Thus the opposite of everlasting life is not everlasting punishment, but death. Oblivion. Nothing. Just not existing.

119

The New Testament relates this threat of death to the fact of our sinfulness. Death is understood as being the consequence of our wrongdoing, our rebellion against God.

Not too many years ago, when I was trying to work my way through the tangle of notions about death, I was quite unable to understand why the New Testament makes such a fuss about death. I was inclined to the apparently reasonable view that death is simply a biological necessity. The continuance of the race depends on the succession of generations. The old ones have to get out of the way to make room for the new ones. This seemed quite logical. And I couldn't understand why the New Testament insists that death is an enemy, a threat, a consequence of our sinfulness.

Then I realized that in the New Testament death means not just the dissolution of the body but the death of the whole person. It isn't just the physical apparatus that passes away, but the whole person disappears into nothingness. Death means separation from God, that is, separation from the source of life. Death means the possibility of being everlastingly lost, in the sense that we are no longer able to live because we are cut off from the ground of our existence. This is the threat of death, the threat of not being, the threat of annihilation, the threat of separation from Life, that is God.

The seriousness of death is dramatized in the notion of hell. Unfortunately, this doctrine has been abused in two directions. Conventional Christianity has interpreted hell to mean everlasting punishment. But this is such an absurd notion that it is discredited by most thoughtful persons and is no longer taken seriously. Consequently, what happens is that the whole idea of hell is dismissed. And it is assumed that there is nothing in our destiny corresponding to the word "hell." There is only "heaven"—whatever that is.

But such a view entirely misses the seriousness of death, which is the intent of the doctrine of hell. The possibility of hell simply means the possibility of eternal death. To be "lost" is to miss the destiny which God intends for us. To be "damned" is to fail to find the fulfillment which God offers. Death is annihilation, because we have cut ourselves off from the only source of life, God.

This is where the New Testament begins. This is why death is an "enemy" of life. It threatens any meaning we might imagine. And it may be some primeval intuition of this threat that lingers in our deep and deeply hidden anxiety about death. In any case, the Christian must reckon with this reality.

The New Testament goes on from this serious view of death to affirm that God is the Lord of life, and that those who commit themselves to him will not perish but will be given eternal life. This divine affirmation of life, however, is not easily or simply made. God asserts his power over death only at great cost. And here the New Testament resorts to a variety of dramatic figures of speech to affirm its meaning. God does not have the power of life over death just because he is God. He must "defeat the enemy." He must "combat the forces of evil." He must "overcome death." And the manifestation of the divine power, with all its costliness, is expressed in the death and resurrection of Jesus Christ. Here is the expression in history of God's eternal affirmation of life, God's power to grant life to those who yield themselves to his purposes for them.

In order to fufill the destiny he intends for us, God comes to us in Christ to assure us of his intention. In order to save us from getting lost, God comes to find us in Christ. In order to release us from the threat of non-being, God manifests his power to give life. In Jesus Christ, God takes upon himself the full cost of our being rescued out of the primitive but pervasive anxiety about death. This is the meaning of the suffering of Christ. In order to break the hold of death on us, God takes into his very being the full threat of nothingness. This is the significance of Christ's death. "He descended into hell." And to manifest his ultimate power of life, God catches up all that agony and all that dreadful threat into a final act of affirmation. This is the meaning of the resurrection. God is the giver of life. And he offers this gift to all who will open themselves to it.

It must be emphasized that the New Testament does not claim that humans are naturally immortal. There is in these Christian documents no teaching of the immortality of the soul. This is a Greek notion which has been lightly baptized and passed off as Christian doctrine. But in the New Testament the emphasis is not upon the inherent power of man but upon the eternal power of God. He wills to share that power with men, to give them the gift of eternal life. And the primitive intuition of this truth is the notion of the immortality of the soul. The intimations of immortality which are scattered through religious and philosophical literature are hints and glimpses of the truth revealed in Jesus Christ. The deepest truth is not the assurance of immortality but the assertion of resurrection. It is because he lives that we hope also to live.

As God brought forth Christ from the dead, so he will bring forth all who belong to him. God is the Creator and Sustainer of life. He is the One who can give life to all who open themselves to this gift. Therefore, in Christ death can be an illusion. Physical death can be a transition into eternal life. God has conquered death and offers us a share in the fruits of his victory.

Death is dead.

ASSERTION OF HOPE

Such a faith gives meaning to our lives. It is an assertion of hope that has implications for our present practice.

The unchanging purpose of God is to give eternal life to his creatures. Our intended destiny is to live as members of his family. To accomplish this purpose, to make possible this destiny, God continually extends his love and power to us. In Christ, God is always affirming his love, always offering his power. The secret of life, then, is for us to accept his love, to yield to his power. For our destiny is achieved only with our consent. As we yield this consent, we live with an increasing sense of fulfillment. This is what God intends us to be. And we live in the confidence that, as our lives are committed to him, God will grant whatever he wills to be our final destiny.

Concerning this destiny we can know relatively little. And it is wise to leave it this way. We may speculate in many interesting ways about life after death. But it is easy to fall into wistful or futile thinking. It is better to leave these matters to God. The one assurance we do have is that every dimension of our personal existence is destined to share in eternal life.

Such an affirmation is strikingly different from any other teaching I know about. The Greeks could only believe in disembodied spirits wandering joylessly through Elysian fields. This is eternal boredom. The Hindu notion of reincarnation destroys the identity of the person. Who is a person when he is reincarnated as an animal? Or else one's identity is lost by absorption into the Infinite. Some of the current adaptations of these notions of immortality are equally questionable, and certainly have little relation to the New Testament insights.

The key to our Christian hope of eternal life is found in Paul's teaching concerning the resurrection of a new body (Cf. I Cor. 15). Our destiny is not to be translated into some vague, disembodied existence, but to be raised into a new dimension of life, equipped with a new body adequate to this new existence. Nor is it the present physical body which is to be reassembled. How Christianity ever became confused at this point I cannot guess. Because the insight of Paul seems perfectly clear and convincing. It is a spiritual body which will be given us for the future adventures of eternity. If we are asked what are the characteristics of this body, we can only say we do not know. We have no direct evidence. It will be as different from our present body as a stalk of corn or of wheat is from the seed which is planted in the ground (Cf. I Cor. 15:35-38). We can simply believe that whatever equipment is needed for the fulfilled life of eternity will be granted us by the God who has shaped us for this destiny.

Some time ago I was in a seminar addressed by a venerable and respected professor of philosophy. He was summarizing a series of lectures he had recently delivered. He came finally to the subject of immortality, and was speculating about it in a fascinating manner. He could not conceive of a disembodied existence, so was driven to consider the possibility of reincarnation. For a moment it seemed as if he were moving toward Paul's conception of a spiritual body. But suddenly he veered away.

In the discussion that followed this was pointed out to him. But for some reason he seemed quite unaware of what was being said. The necessity of some kind of embodiment he could sense. But why he was attracted to the vague intuitions of the East rather than to the sharp insights of Paul, I do not know. He simply did not see that Paul is staking out a claim which commands not only the assent of faith but commends itself to honest intellectual evaluation.

Every dimension of our personal existence is destined to share in eternal life. The whole person will be raised up to a new life of fellowship and service with God and one another, in the life of increasing fulfillment which we call "heaven."

This hopeful faith is not just an expectation for the future but is a source of strength for the present. "The power of the resurrection" is an immediate resource for faithful living. The same divine power by which God raised Christ from the dead is available to us for raising us above our present frustrations and failures. God's victory over death is the promise of our increasing victory over the powers which cause the little deaths of our daily anxieties and fears.

God has conquered death. Therefore, he can make us truly alive, fully alive. We can be delivered from anxiety about death, and anxiety about all the threats to life. We need not be haunted by nameless fears; we can know hope and assurance and confidence. We belong to God. We can never be completely alone again. Therefore, we may tentatively reach out to others to discover new relations of reconciliation, of fellowship in Christ.

We become new persons, sustained by a purpose, given to a meaning, headed for a destiny. We know ourselves to be linked with other persons so sustained and directed. And we all know ourselves to be sustained and guided by the God who manifests his love for us in Jesus Christ and shares his power with us through that same Christ.

This is the meaning of the resurrection.

Our hope has never been more fittingly and beautifully expressed than by John, in his first letter (3:2): "Beloved, we are God's children *now*, it does not yet appear what we shall be, but we know that when he appears we shall be like him, for we shall see him as he is."